MAGIC AUSTRALIA

The publisher would like to thank the author's children, Tess and Chris Horwitz, for agreeing to bring this book back into print and for their edits to the text.

1.0.1 This revised edition published 2017

By Living Book Press

147 Durren Rd, Jilliby, 2259

Text and images Copyright © The Estate of Nuri Mass (1943 and 2017)

Text edits by Tess Horwitz and Chris Horwitz

All rights reserved. No part of this publication may be reproduced, stored in a retrieval system, or transmitted in any other form or means – electronic, mechanical, photocopying, recording or otherwise, without the prior permission of the copyright owner and the publisher or as provided by Australian law.

National Library of Australia Cataloguing-in-Publication entry:

Creator:	Mass, Nuri
Title:	Magic Australia / by Nuri Mass ; illustrated by Celeste Mass.
ISBN:	9780648063339 (hardback)
	9780648035602 (paperback)
Target Audience:	For primary school age.
Subjects:	Magic--Juvenile fiction.
	Adventure stories, Australian.
Other Creators/ Contributors:	Mass, Celeste, illustrator.

Children's books by the same author and artist

AUSTRALIAN WILD FLOWER FAIRIES
THE LITTLE GRAMMAR PEOPLE
THE WIZARD OF JENOLAN

Children's books by the same author

AUSTRALIAN WILDFLOWER MAGIC
THE WONDERLAND OF NATURE
FLOWERS OF THE AUSTRALIAN ALPS

A lonely little figure in the shade of a pandanus palm.

MAGIC AUSTRALIA

By
NURI MASS

Illustrated by
CELESTE MASS

LIVING BOOK PRESS
2017

FOREWORD

Nuri's children, Chris Horwitz and Tess Horwitz, think that when Nuri wrote about Del, the main character in this book, she may have been remembering a young relative that she grew up with for a time in Argentina's big city of Buenos Aires. Nuri had no sister or brother, so he was the only boy she knew and she always recalled him as being difficult. In this book Nuri brings him to a new life in Australia and shows him learning to love the natural world about him, and to treat others with respect.

Nuri Mass was only 26 years of age when she wrote *Magic Australia*. In the book's story-line Nuri reflected the beliefs of the Second World War period in history. The book gave prominence to the vision of Human Industry tapping nature's bounties to enable progress for "millions upon millions of people" by damming rivers and mining nature's "treasures".

By the time Nuri had reached middle age she no longer held this belief, in fact she was a passionate campaigner for reducing human intervention in nature and for protecting the wisdom of natural cycles. So, for example, with the damming of the great northern rivers, Nuri learned over time that this would create environmental disasters by preventing the flooding patterns that both create rich soil and enable whole habitats, like waterbirds, to flourish.

We have edited this version of *Magic Australia* to better align with Nuri's later beliefs; the story remains one full of passion for the unrivalled beauty and great adventure that Australia offers us all.

TO MY MOTHER

For one whose joy is, life right through,
Her all to give;
Who makes the sweetest things come true,
And magic live.

Magic, when thy spell is cast
O'er the heart of man or child,
Is there aught that, willing, might—
Age, or scorn, or noonday light—
Stay thy wanderings wild?

Magic, oh to flame e'en once
By thy side like shooting star
And, beyond the pall that clings,
Mortalizing, over things,
See them as they are!

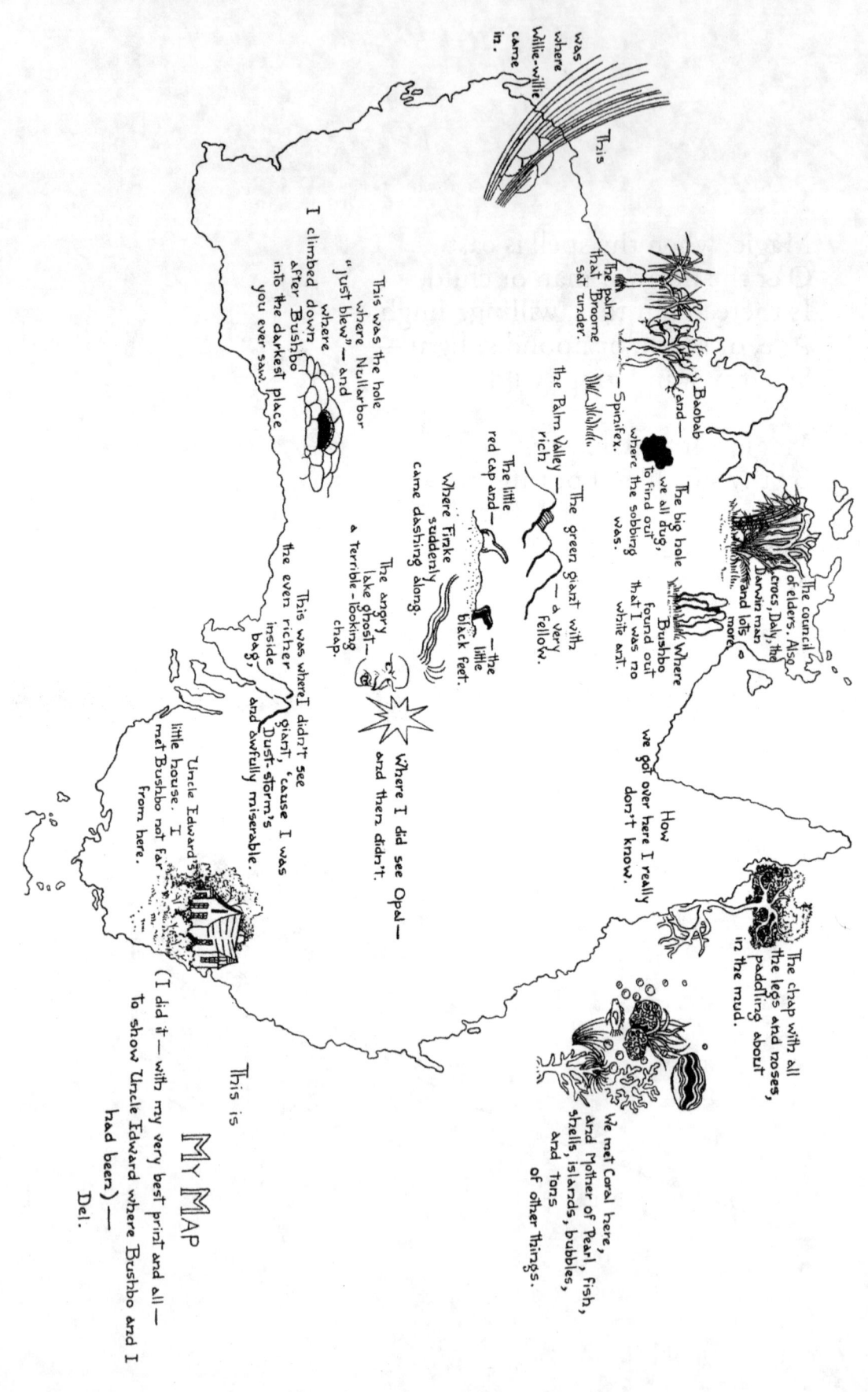

CONTENTS

CHAPTER		PAGE
I.	UNCLE EDWARD	1
II.	THE BUSH BOY	5
III.	WILLIE-WILLIE	11
IV.	LANDED!	20
V.	THE GRASS MAN	31
VI.	TERRORS AND TEARS	41
VII.	THE GREEN GIANT	49
VIII.	THE LITTLE RED DESERT PEA OF MEMORY LAND	59
IX.	CAUGHT!	71
X.	DARTING FLAME	83
XI.	THE PALACE OF NULLARBOR	88
XII.	THE CORAL KINGDOM	102
XIII.	OVER THE REEF	115
XIV.	THE WIDE-AWAKE DREAM	126
XV.	THE COUNCIL OF ELDERS	135
XVI.	FOUND!	144
	IN OTHER WORDS	155

CHAPTER I

UNCLE EDWARD

DEL was only nine years old and a day when he had that adventure which he declares to this very hour to have been the most wonderful in his life.

He and his father were spending a long week-end with his Uncle Edward at the time—a thing Del loved doing perhaps more than any other.

Uncle Edward had retired from his work in the city a few years before, and had bought an exciting little house in one of the prettiest parts along the coast south from Sydney—a little house that he had soon filled and surrounded with all manner of interesting things. Outside it he grew a large and beautiful garden, and inside it he was for ever carpentering and inventing. Then, he had his many collections —of shells and corals, of favourite books, of ancient coins and, strangely enough, amongst many others, of smoking pipes. Del loved this last collection perhaps best of all, for each pipe was so real a character and many of them were so quaint that at times they seemed to have something quite elfish about them.

Later, of course, Del supposed—and rightly enough—that what his father and Uncle Edward had been talking about over the breakfast table on that never-to-be-forgotten morning had had a good bit to do with all that followed; had taken the form of magic watchwords, actually, opening the gates of his mind self and making him able to see and hear far more than he could during the awake hours of his mortal self in the Monday-to-Sunday world.

They had been talking, he remembered, about Australia. Even now he could recall their conversation almost word for word.

"Terrible drought!" his father had said. "Any one would think this was the Centre instead of the south-east."

Uncle Edward had grunted; then, after a long silence, had remarked, "Wonderful country, though—the most wonderful on earth. That's my opinion. Unique—absolutely unique. Ask the scientists."

"True," Del's father had agreed.

"Why?" Del himself had asked. "What's wrong with it?"

"Nothing's wrong with it, old chap. It's just different, that's all."

"Well, but how different, uncle?"

"Now, that is a long story, my lad, and we certainly haven't got time to go into it this morning. Let's see, it must go back thousands, perhaps millions of years. I don't remember back as far as that. Anyway, a few ages before those odd creatures called boys and girls were even thought of—" Uncle Edward always had such a nice way of putting things—"also before Australia fell out with Asia and America—"

"Fell out?"

"Why yes. Haven't you ever heard about that? The ocean came between them."

He came to the little rustic gate.

MAGIC AUSTRALIA

"Oh!" Del had looked a good bit puzzled, and Uncle Edward had ruffled his hair and laughed.

Then the conversation had continued again without him, and he could not remember this part so well afterwards, except that quite a lot had been said about opals and many other precious stones; gold, silver and many other valuable metals; about all the marvellous corals and shells in the Great Barrier Reef up north, where most of Uncle Edward's collection had come from, and about the pearls of the north-west; about an enormous amount of underground water—artesian, they had called it—and, among lots of other things, about the animals and plants of Australia, so different from those of every other country.

Then gradually, other things were talked about, and Australia —that strange land of wonder and mystery—seemed to have been forgotten; but not by Del. He kept on thinking and thinking, and asking himself a thousand hows, whys and whens. And as his father's and Uncle Edward's talk kept interrupting and confusing him, he slipped outside into the garden, and walked in and out amongst the bright flowery plots, pulling off a leaf here and kicking a pebble there, until he came to the little rustic gate. He opened this, and wandered out on to a narrow track, which sidled off into the most out-of-the-way and interesting places. And it was then that all the wonderful things began to happen.

CHAPTER II

THE BUSH BOY

SUDDENLY, after he had been walking for only a few minutes, Del found himself on the top of a cliff he did not remember having seen before, and right at its edge.

Down below—by leaning over ever so carefully he could just see them—there were big blue waves crashing up quickly, one after the other, on to huge rocks. All of them looked very stately, for they each wore a snow-white crown which, in the moment that it lasted, frothed and sprayed like a fairy fountain.

Far out beyond, there was one enormous stretch of the deepest blue imaginable. It looked as if it must go on for ever and ever; and the sunlight fell upon it in millions of sparkles.

Del was entranced, and stood quite still there on the cliff edge for many minutes. He knew it was only the giant ocean he was gazing at, yet to-day somehow, it looked different from what it had ever looked like before. It seemed strangely alive, as if it might at any moment rear up a huge head and speak to him—a head covered with streaming blue hair and encircled with a band of sunlight and foam.

Then he turned to look back upon the thick, many-coloured bush that rose up in hills and spread itself out in broad flat stretches behind him, and, to his astonishment, he found that he was not alone. Coming towards him with a bold, free step was a boy several years older than himself, of slight though powerful build, with skin golden-brown in colour, and heavy locks of dark brown hair that flashed with lightning streaks of gold and copper as the sun struck upon it. He wore a strange moss-green garment something like the leopard-skin of

MAGIC AUSTRALIA

shepherds, and his feet were sandalled with what seemed to be the interwoven fine, strong tendrils of climbing plants.

Del, when he saw him, started with surprise, then stood quite still, eyeing the stranger with a mixture of curiosity and suspicion, wondering what right he had in this part of the world that Del had just discovered for himself, and why on earth the boy was dressed like that.

Finally the newcomer brushed aside a sprig of tea-tree and stood only about a yard off. "Hullo!" he said, smiling, and with a kind and gentle voice.

"Hullo!" Del replied. "Who are you?"

The other looked thoughtful for a moment, then shrugged his shoulders carelessly. "Oh, no one in particular—just general bush boy."

This answer puzzled Del rather, and, in his anxiety to hide the fact, he asked sharply, "And what are you doing here, anyway?"

Again the boy smiled—a trifle sadly—then

It seemed strangely alive.

replied, "I thought you wouldn't take long to ask that, little white one."

"Why?" Del demanded, feeling uncomfortable.

"Oh, because that is what white ones have always done right from the beginning. When they came first to this great and priceless storehouse of nature, it mattered nothing to them that the dark people of the bush and desert had known it as their home for hundreds of years past, and just like that—" here the bush boy snapped his fingers, and the call of a whip-bird echoed piercingly through the clear air—"yes, just like that," he continued, "the white ones claimed everything for themselves, and made the gentle dark people their slaves, taking their home and freedom from them, even their thoughts; asking them what right they had to be here—"

Del's eyes lit up. He knew something about this. He had often heard Uncle Edward speaking of it. "Yes," he said, highly pleased with himself, "those were the aborigines. I've seen pictures of them. Uncle Edward's got a big book all about them, and I look at it sometimes. Well then, I s'pose you're an aborigine too—although," he added a little less boastfully, "you don't much look like one."

"No," answered the boy, "I'm not one of them, but I'm their friend."

Del thrust his hands into his pockets, and started unconcernedly scraping a groove into the soft earth with his foot. "Then I s'pose you don't like white men," he declared at last.

The bush boy gave a sudden laugh, which was immediately repeated high up in a nearby gumtree by a merry-hearted kookaburra. "Oh yes I do," he said. "I'm their friend too. They're not all of them unkind."

"*I'm* not," Del was rather surprised to hear himself saying after a slight pause.

"I sort of guessed you weren't," said the bush boy.

And that being settled, Del, with no apparent concern, took

out a horn-handled pocket-knife, which Uncle Edward had given him for his birthday, and began cutting his initials into the trunk of a sapling gum with it.

"What do you do that for?" the bush boy asked.

"Oh, I don't know," Del replied, somewhat absently. "Just for fun. Why? Don't you ever do it?"

"No, I don't. If I wanted to write my name anywhere I think I'd want to do it in a useful way."

"What do you mean?" Del asked, looking up with clear interest, his knife suddenly arrested half-way along a downward stroke. "What sort of a useful way? And what is your name, anyhow?"

Repeated by a merry-hearted kookaburra.

"My name? Oh, I don't know. I've never thought of it. Nothing special, I suppose. I'm just the bush boy, that's all."

"All right then, Bushbo," said Del with a broad grin. "But what sort of a useful way would you write it in if you did have one?"

The bush boy folded his arms and was silent for a few moments. He gazed around him at the small wild flowers spangling the earth, at the numbers of scrubby bushes about then up at the tall, crescent-leafed gums. "It's hard to explain," he answered. "I dare say I'd try to help plants grow and animals live in all of these places. But first I'd have to speak with the wind and rain and heat and other spirits, for without their help I couldn't do anything much."

Del, by this time, was frankly mystified. He gazed wide-eyed, then slowly scratched at the back of his head, just as Uncle Edward always did when he felt uncertain about anything.

"Look, what are you talking about?" he said at last. Then suddenly he flushed, and added hotly, "I-I don't know what you think I'm made of, to believe in your stupid ghosts and fairies. I'm not a baby! I'm not scared!"

But Bushbo only smiled at him a trifle pityingly. "It's wonderful," he said, "how human beings struggle to keep blind and deaf and feelingless, when they've got such huge powers hidden inside them somewhere—far richer than all the countless treasures that the earth spirit holds locked away from men's sight. Ah well. I was mistaken, that's all. I thought you wanted me." And with this, he turned and strode away through the bushes.

Del watched him for a few seconds, uncertain what to do. Then suddenly he closed his pen-knife and thrust it into his pocket, jerked his head up into the air and marched off whistling a tune. But he only went where he could see the boy's retreating figure a little longer—rich golden-brown and moss-green, the sunlight flickering over it like a thousand caressing finger-tips.

At last he could stand it no longer and, "Hey, Bushbo!" he shouted, running towards him as fast as the springy branches sprawling out around him in all directions would let him. "Where are you going?"

The golden-brown boy stopped, turned and waited; then, as Del caught up with him, slightly puffed, "I hardly thought you'd be interested," he said. "Aren't you afraid of being scared?"

Del gave him a playful push. "Aw, go on!" he exclaimed. "I was only joking. Be a sport. Tell us where you're going."

"That's a fairly long story," Bushbo replied after a pause.

"And besides, I don't think you'd care about it much. You'd better go along home."

"But I don't *want* to go home," Del cried petulantly. "And what's more. I'm not *going* home. I'm coming with you."

Bushbo looked down at him uncertainly for a moment, then shrugged his shoulders and sighed. "Well, if you must you must, I s'pose," he declared. "But mind now, I didn't ask you to come, so if you don't like it don't blame me!"

And with this he turned and continued on his way, taking long even strides, while Del tramped doggedly beside him, never speaking a word, tripping every now and then over the wiry entanglement of some creeping plant, and whittling a branch of tea-tree with his handsome new pen-knife as he went.

CHAPTER III

WILLIE-WILLIE

WHEN the two boys had been travelling in this way for what seemed to have been several hours, and the sun was high up in the sky and the day had grown very bright and hot, Del stopped abruptly in the meagre shade of a few massed-together, light bushes and cried out, "Look here, Bushbo, how much longer is this going on?"

"That's just what I've been wondering," the bush boy replied, seeming considerably peeved and all of a sudden sitting down on the soft, sandy soil, hoisting his knees up chin-high and clasping his hands around them. "Why on earth don't you let yourself go, Del?"

"What do you mean? Let myself go where?"

"Where we *are* going, of course—or *would* be, if you'd only let us."

Del looked rather indignant. "What am I doing to stop us? That's what I'd like to know. Look here, Bushbo, you've gone and lost us, that's what; and now you're trying to palm the blame off on to me."

But the bush boy's only answer was a weary sigh, as he rested his chin on his knees and gazed out across the wide stretch of surrounding flat country.

For a few minutes Del strutted about undecidedly, kicking pebbles, scratching lines into the sand with a grass-stick he had collected on the way, and doing a vast amount of grumbling on the subject of being hot, tired and thirsty. Then finally he threw himself down flat on his back in a sprinkle of shade beside Bushbo, and clasped his hands together under his head.

"I'm going to have a sleep," he announced, shortly. "And by the time I wake up, Bushbo, I hope you'll be able to tell me some way to get us out of this."

And he had scarcely finished speaking before his eyelids sank down and he was fast asleep. But the bush boy, who had long been awaiting something like this, was suddenly more wide awake than ever and, giving a chuckle of delight, sprang up like a long-legged grasshopper, and got busy without wasting a moment.

When Del woke up again after only a very few minutes, he thought for a second or two that he must still be dreaming, for the queerest thing in the world had happened. There were strands and billows and cobwebby things all around him, and everything—himself as well—seemed to be moving at a terrific rate. But, he wondered with a sudden start, where? And how? What on earth could have happened between the moment he fell asleep and now to make everything so queer and different, and to make it almost seem as if—

"Heavens! Hey, Bushbo, wh-what's the jolly idea?" he cried out shrilly, taking a quick look all round, and seeing that he was actually not on the ground at all, but far, far above it. And that he was being carried along by the merest ribbony wisps of clouds, far too thin and light to hold a couple of white rabbits, let alone a lusty young man just nine years old.

"Hey, Bushbo!" he shouted again, through the loud rushing noise that seemed to be following him everywhere. And he called even a little more shrilly this time, for his green and brown friend had not replied, and indeed was nowhere to be seen, and Del was now properly frightened about everything.

However, Bushbo's cheery voice was not long in coming, and suddenly his curly brown hair and bright eyes popped up near by over one of the many tall mountains of floating net, followed by his whole scrambling self. "Well, hullo! What's the matter with you? Managed to wake up at last, I see!"

He called even a little more shrilly this time.

Del, wild with excitement and relief, plunged out towards him, but only fell face downward into a heap of cobwebbiness, which seemed to amuse the bush boy very much, for the whole flying world rang with his merry laughter.

Scrambling and puffing, Del at last managed to find his feet again, but he stood uncertainly on them and looked very uncomfortable indeed. "Look here, Bushbo, I—I'm all sort of mixed up about things."

The bush boy chuckled. "Yes," he said, "I suppose you are, rather. Well, you see, we were getting along quite nicely—going round the edge, you know—"

"No," Del broke in, "I don't know at all. *What* edge?"

"The edge of Australia. The one opposite the one you went to sleep on a few moments ago, of course. That was the eastern edge, so this other was the western one. See?"

Del looked as if he did not see in the least, and he tried again to get a little closer, for all this shouting above the loud rushing noise was an awful nuisance, to put it mildly. But he only tumbled over much the same as before, and Bushbo laughed louder than ever.

"Why don't you hold on to something?" he asked. "That might help you to keep right way up."

So Del, with a little grunt, did what he had thought until now would seem quite ridiculous and, grabbing a handful of cloud, steadied himself by it.

"Ah!" said Bushbo. "That's better. Now we may be able to carry on a sensible conversation. Well, as I was saying, we were getting along quite nicely when Willie-willie came tearing in from the sea, and—well, here we are."

"But—but that's just the point," Del insisted, stamping his foot down into the light billows to show that he really meant what he was saying. "*Who's* Willie-willie, and *where* are we?"

"Haven't the faintest idea where we are, old chap," Bushbo answered airily. "But Willie-willie—now, surely that marvellous Uncle Edward of yours has told you about him."

WILLIE-WILLIE

And Del was just about to declare that Uncle Edward had never so much as mentioned the fellow's name when he nearly jumped out of his skin with surprise, for suddenly there was a long, stretched-out sort of face, that seemed to have no end anywhere, staring straight at him, and doing something that looked very much like smiling—though one could never be sure, of course.

"And—and who on earth are *you*?" Del shouted, feeling that, for some reason or other, everything was conspiring to puzzle and worry him.

Doing something that looked very much like smiling.

"Aha!" answered the face, and then again, "Aha!" with a swishing kind of voice. And it smiled more broadly, until its mouth looked exactly like a great half-moon, and its eyes shot electric sparks of mischief about all over the place. And then it turned away once more with a quick, streaming movement, and the next moment Del and Bushbo were being treated to a mad spin—round, round, until neither of them knew for certain where any part of himself was. But when it was all over and they were speeding forward in a simple straight line again, Del found himself rolled up into a little ball at Bushbo's feet.

He looked up curiously, and Bushbo, with a wide grin. leaned down and whispered right into his ear, "Willie-willie!"

"Oh!" breathed Del, much impressed.

"And what do you think *you* are, anyway?" the bush boy added. "Hedgehog? Funny-looking woolly grub? Caterpillar?"

Del quickly picked himself up at that—so quickly, in fact, that he nearly threw himself out over the edge of what he had by now decided must be some sort of wind chariot, and, had Bushbo not grabbed hold of his trouser legs in the nick of time, he would certainly have gone spinning down to earth as fast as a shooting star, and landed on the tip of his nose; and there our story might well have ended.

Instead of that, Bushbo saw to it that he stayed right where he was. But before the whole of him was dragged back again, Del saw something that gave him plenty to think and talk about for ages to come. Below him were what he thought to be any amount of great flying loops and streamers all of the same stuff as the chariot he and Bushbo were riding in. Then suddenly, while he was watching and wondering, a long grey-coloured arm shot down through them with, at the end of it, a thin hand so huge that its fingers looked like the shadows of sunrays spreading out across the earth.

Del had no more than two or three seconds to wonder what the idea was when those giant fingers stretched down to the very ground, snapped together around a whole house and threw it up towards him as if it were no heavier than a football. It did not quite reach him, though, before it got caught into one of the swaying loops and, rolling about there all askew, went sailing along in the most undignified positions imaginable.

"Say, Bushbo!" Del cried out, highly excited, when his friend

WILLIE-WILLIE

had hauled him back again into safety. "If only you'd seen that! Great Scott, fancy catching houses in nets, instead of butterflies! Nets—oh, but heavens! I've never even dreamt of such big nets. And—and Willie-willie's hand—wow!" he squeaked, and for the moment could think of absolutely nothing else to say.

"Yes, I know all about that," Bushbo laughed, "and I s'pose you think it's great fun. But it isn't, really—not quite. Willie-willie's a very bad fellow, I'm afraid. He thinks it's a huge joke rooting things up and throwing them about, but he doesn't consider any one else's feelings, and sometimes he does the cruellest things under the sun—even kills people. I'll never forgive him for some of the things he's done, and every one who lives in the north-west of Australia is scared to death of him, I can tell you."

"Gracious!" Del breathed, very seriously. "And does he come along just at any old time?"

"No. He comes in from the sea, with the summer monsoons—great strong winds that, when they're in a Willie-willieish mood, upset everything and every one, and do mighty little good anywhere that I can think of."

And now came an enormous swish of laughter that sounded almost unreal and ghostly, although it swept backwards and forwards and up and down all around the two boys in gust upon gust of jollity.

"Come on," said Bushbo. "Let's see what he's feeling so pleased with himself about."

So they both lay flat down together on their tummies, and peered through the floor of their chariot at the large, sandy-looking world below them, and they were just in time to see a few hundred yards of somebody's fence being snatched up by Willie-willie's strong fingers and hurled into one of his streaming nets.

Del positively gurgled with wonder and delight at this display of power, but Bushbo looked very solemn; and even more so a few minutes later when Willie-willie made off with a number of sheep and cows, and even a man or two, and tore up an old woman's garden.

"Look! Oh, look!" cried Del, pointing down at a group of houses chained to the ground with thick cables just as if they were boats that might drift away down some river at any moment.

But even as he pointed, Willie-willie's fingers folded round them and, with enormous strength, he pushed and tugged at them until up they came bounding, cables and all, one after another.

"Heavens!" Del exclaimed, glancing round at the huge net

Peered through at the world below them.

chariots which seemed to be covering every bit of space there was, and all of which were quite weighed down with the loads they were carrying. "What a bag! Say, Bushbo, I think we must have a good few whole towns up here by this time."

"I shouldn't be a bit surprised," the bush boy agreed. "Willie-willie's got no conscience at all, the old villain."

"Yes, he *is* rather rough, but—well, it is a bit of fun too, you know. I mean," Del added, "houses and fences and farms, and

WILLIE-WILLIE

animals and people and gardens and things all dashing about in the air—say, I've never even *thought* of anything so funny." And, without being able to help it, he wriggled and chuckled with excitement. But Bushbo only smiled rather faintly.

"What I'd like to know," Del went on, "is what he's going to do with us all. He can't keep whisking us about like this for ever."

"No," said Bushbo, "he'll have to get tired before long, and then he'll just drop us about here and there wherever he likes. And my word, you heartless little brute," he added with a twinkle, "it would serve you jolly well right if he took you out and dropped you in the sea."

CHAPTER IV

LANDED!

BUT Willie-willie did nothing of the kind. He had grown quite fond of Del while rushing him about all over the sky, and so, choosing a nice sandy beach laced about with wiry grasses, and twinkling in the sunshine with flakes and splinters of mother-of-pearl just as the sky at night-time does with stars, he went sweeping down to it in one long dive; and when he got there, suddenly, before either of the boys had any idea of what was happening, he tipped their great net chariot upside down, and out they both tumbled, rolling over and over along the sand and mother-of-pearl, while he, shouting and whirling with the loudest wind laughter possible, went circling up again into endless space.

"Say, look here, Bushbo," Del exclaimed at last, with dizzy head and merry eyes, "I haven't been knocked about so much all my life as I have been since I met you. What's the matter with everything?"

But Bushbo's only reply to this was a laugh, cut short in the middle by his catching sight of a lonely little figure sitting quite still not far away, on the edge of a sandy headland and in the shade of a ragged pandanus palm. "Look!" he whispered.

So Del looked, and blinked hard lots of times, and kept on looking. What, he was wondering, could it possibly be, staying so still for such a long time? A person? A ghost of a person? A marble statue, perhaps, like those way back in the Sydney Museum and Art Gallery?

"That," said Bushbo, "is Broome. Come and let's have a few words with her."

LANDED!

"You—you can talk to her, then?" Del asked.

"Of course. Why shouldn't you be able to?"

"Oh, I don't know. She's sitting so still, I wondered if she was real."

"Of course she's real; but surely you wouldn't expect a town to get up and walk about at any old time."

"No, but she's not a town, silly! Towns are made of streets and houses and things."

Bushbo laughed. "Are they, indeed! And nothing else, I s'pose. It's time you learnt a thing or two about the places human beings carry on their lives in, old chap."

Del waited for some further explanation; then, as none came, "Oh, look here, I do wish you wouldn't talk riddles," he burst out. "What on earth *has* she got to do with a town, anyway?"

"Why, she's its spirit, of course," Bushbo replied simply.

As the two boys had been ambling along towards her all this time, being almost chirped and twittered to now and then by an occasional wandering tree thick with throngs of green and yellow bird flowers as beaky and cheeky as any real birds could be, they had now nearly reached her, and Del thought her one of the loveliest things he had ever seen. Sitting there with her knees drawn up nearly to her chin and her white hands with pearly finger-nails clasped around them, she was gazing far out over the wide sea as if she would never do anything else right through the whole of time. Her hair fell to her shoulders in soft, golden waves, and was threaded through with a string of shining pearls. She had a necklace of pearls, and a girdle of them too, and one little bracelet and one anklet. And her dress, golden with here and there a lightning streak of vivid red, looked exactly like a poinciana flower.

"Hail, Broome!" Bushbo cried out cheerily.

The lovely creature turned slowly, and smiled at him. "Hail, Eastern Bushlands!" she answered.

Del was highly excited by this form of greeting, and assured himself he simply must remember all about it to tell Uncle Edward when he got home again. "Oh," he declared, "this *is* fun—the best ever. I never dreamt any one could see a town looking like this and—and talk to it and everything. But say, Broome, don't you ever get sick of sitting just here in the one spot for the whole of your life?"

"Sick of it?" she repeated. "No, of course not. Why should I?"

"Oh, I don't know. It would drive me silly, though, I think, just staring out at the sea all day with nothing else to do."

"Ah, but there you are mistaken," she answered softly, "for where there is a living spirit there is no such thing as idleness. There are all my people to shelter, and their lives to stand guardian over, and there are any amount of joys, and many worries too."

"What are some of the joys?" Del asked.

Little fairy lanterns, prettier than the stars.

"Oh, lots of things—seeing their gay festivals with many-coloured gowns and paper flowers in the daytime, and little fairy lanterns all over the land and sea at night, prettier than the stars; watching over the play and love of my young people, and the birth of little children, and the courage of my grown-up men who spend their whole lives diving for pearls—diving, diving, year in, year out, always for pearls, and for the satiny

LANDED!

moonlight shells they live and grow in, these prettiest gems of Mother Sea."

She hesitated here, so Del, anxious to hear her talk more and more in her soft, singing voice, quickly asked, "And—and your worries, then—what would some of those be?"

And now her face grew very sad as she replied, "Ah, the worries—when my brave divers are attacked or eaten by cruel sharks, or are drawn up from the bottom of the sea all stiff and tortured with a terrible cramp; or when Willie-willie the great hurricane teases and jostles Mother Sea about until she gets angry and drowns them, and dashes their little boats to pieces, while he rushes up to the township and blows their homes away, and while I—I who love them—can do nothing except sit here on the headland and watch—"

"Oh, I say then," Del broke in, "you must have been terribly upset just now when Bushbo and I came along—with Willie-willie."

"Yes," she sighed. "Ah yes! But other times have been far worse. After all, he only touched here this time, and didn't stop to root things about the way he often does. In fact, he's really never, I dare say, treated me as badly as he might have. Just think of my sister towns Roebourne, Cossack and Onslow, for instance, who live farther down on the map than I do. Poor little Roebourne has had everything belonging to her blown right away by Willie-willie fifteen times, and Cossack eleven times, and Onslow nine. And those are only three. There are lots and lots more."

And pretty little Broome, with her poinciana frock and her strings of pearls, looked suddenly so sad that Del was sorry he had asked her about the worries of a north-west Australian town. But, just as he was about to change the subject to something happier, Willie-willie's rushing laughter burst out once more way up in the sky, and came swishing down towards him with, at the same time, the huge grey net Del remembered so clearly.

MAGIC AUSTRALIA

It was, certainly, great fun speeding through the air in a wind chariot and seeing the world below as small as a doll's playground, and feeling Willie-willie's power; but Del was only angry with the old monster now—as angry as could be—so he sat down hard on the sand and snapped and scowled.

"Oh, go away, you! Go away, you horrid thing!" he shouted. "I don't like you any more."

But Willie-willie only laughed more than ever at that, and Bushbo assured him that "It's no use, old chap. Might as well go without any fuss. Remember, he might tip you out into the middle of the sea."

And he had hardly finished saying this when they were both swung off the ground and whisked up into the air once more in Willie-willie's all-catching net, leaving Broome, small and lonely, still sitting there on the edge of the map, with her bright, hot sunshine and her milk-white pearls. And Del, for one, had not nearly finished talking to her, and was mightily annoyed at being tumbled up and down all over the place like this whether he liked it or not, and altogether what he would have enjoyed more than anything at that moment would have been to give Willie-willie a taste of his own medicine.

Willie-willie, however, was no longer in the tearing good form he had been in at first. Now, when he came to a village, he merely dived down, grabbed it by the shoulders and gave it a thorough shaking instead of lifting it up bit by bit and carrying it away with him; and neither was he travelling nearly as quickly as before. And so it was that Del and Bushbo were able to meet Baobab when they did—that great, rugged, kindly wizard who haunts the north-west and always keeps a cheery welcome stored in his trunk and branches for any one who may pass his way. This was how it happened.

"I tell you, Bushbo, I'm bored," Del announced, rolling over on to his tummy and staring down at the earth, now not so far below him and, as much as he could see of it, all fairly dry and

LANDED!

sandy, with short scrubby bushes and a lot of hard grass, and here and there a tallish tree.

"That's a funny thing," said Bushbo, throwing himself down beside him and also peering over, "because I'm not too happy about things myself. Where *I* want to go is right through into the great sandy and stony Centre—"

"Centre of what?" Del broke in.

"Of Australia, of course, where trees and flowers can't live and are even afraid to try to, because of all the savage tribes there."

"Savage tribes?" Del repeated under his breath, his eyes wide with surprise and excitement. "Tribes of what? Aborigines?"

"No, no," said Bushbo. "The Aboriginal people love the earth's growing things, and are kind to them and make good use of them wherever they find them. No, I meant the fiery heat tribes, war-dancing all over the place and burning to death anything that tries to live there, and the treacherous sand tribes who lie in wait for the rain sprites and pounce out upon them and imprison them far, far down in the earth, where the little searching roots of plants can't reach them—"

"Great Scott!" Del exclaimed. Then, with a spasm of admiration for the older boy, he asked, "And that's why you want to go, Bushbo, to—to fight the tribes or something?"

"Well, to make them see reason and come to some sort of terms, if possible," Bushbo answered.

"And don't you think Willie-willie might take us there?"

"He might, and he could, but on the other hand he might not. He'll only ever please himself."

"Well then, I don't like him," Del shouted at the top of his voice. "I don't like him a bit, and I jolly well want to get down. Help, someone! I want to get down."

"Yes," Bushbo agreed, copying Del and laughing. "Help, someone! I want to get down too!"

And now it was that the most unexpected thing happened.

MAGIC AUSTRALIA

Two long, twisted, brown arms shot up from the top of one of the tallish trees they were passing, and grabbed them right out of Willie-willie's net. It was the queerest and most upsetting

Swung Del down to have a look at him.

feeling, suddenly being snatched out in mid air from the only thing lying between them and a nasty fall, and for a moment or two they were both quite shaken and dazed; but soon a deep kindly chuckle reassured them, and they started to look round and take an intelligent interest in what had happened to them.

LANDED!

And there they were, each gripped firmly in one of old Baobab's brown, twisted, knuckly hands.

"'Heavens!" cried Del. "Heavens alive!" And made such a jump that Baobab had to give an extra squeeze to keep hold of him.

"Oh, my extremely shivering timbers!" he burst out with deep-throated merriment. "I thought I'd caught a boy—not a slippery eel."

And with this he swung Del down on a level with his eyes, just to have a look and make sure; and Del as nearly as anything sprang free again then, for he found himself suddenly face to face with—why, with a talking gargoyle, surely. Uncle Edward had often told him about gargoyles. and had shown him lots of pictures of them in some of his wonderful books—the ugliest, most misshapen hobgoblin sort of things imaginable, that people in the olden days used to carve out of stone and set into all kinds of odd corners in their castles and palaces.

"Heavens alive!" Del breathed once more, turning first very pale and then almost purple. "Are—are you a g-g-gargoyle, sir?" he stammered.

At which Baobab made such a face that he looked more like one than ever. "Indeed!" he rumbled, a good-natured smile twisting his mouth into a funny shape. "You wouldn't, by any chance, be trying to pay me a compliment, young man?"

"Oh y-yes, certainly!" said Del, his heart throbbing away like the engine of his father's motor-car.

"That's a good thing for you," said Baobab, and gave him a playful shake that made him feel very much like an egg flip. "No, I'm not a gargoyle, as it happens. I'm Baobab—friend to anything in the shape of small boys. And now let's see what we've got in the other hand." And he drew Bushbo down and had a look at him.

"Hail, Baobab!" said Bushbo, smiling happily.

"Ah, the eastern bushlands boy!" cried Baobab. "Well, well, well, you *are* welcome, you two. It's many a long month since any traveller passed this way. A terrible business for human beings the summer can be up here. Yes, yes, a terrible business."

"It would be thousands of times worse for them without you, good old Baobab," Bushbo said.

At which the tree made a queer, wry face. "Don't know, I'm sure, why you should call me old. True enough, I've been living a few hundred years, but I'll most likely go on for another few hundred exactly the same, and I can assure you I feel as sprightly as a sapling, what with not the least disposition to wear out, and not even any white ants villainous enough to bother me."

"A few hundred years!" Del gasped.

Baobab laughed. "And by the look of *you*, young man, you wouldn't be able to live out here for longer than a couple of days."

And indeed, having once turned purple, Del had remained so, and little rivers of perspiration were running down all over him, and his throat was so parched that it felt as if it had not seen water for a week.

"Dear me, dear me!" Baobab continued. "We must do something about this. Come now, in you go!"

"In where?" Del asked feebly.

"Why, in me, of course."

"What?" Del squeaked. "Are you going to swallow me, then?"

Which amused kindly old Baobab very much indeed; but instead of answering him, he stooped down and gently set him on the ground at his roots, and Bushbo beside him, and then Del saw that his trunk was an enormous hollow one, and gratefully he bounded straight into it.

"Glory!" he shouted, and his voice echoed strangely in the emptiness. "Say, Bushbo, it's as big as a house. People could live in it."

"Of course," said Bushbo. "And they do live in it from time to time. Look at all the names scratched into the walls."

LANDED!

So Del looked, and sure enough, there was hardly one inch of those rough, woody inside walls not covered with names and initials and written stories and poems and messages. When he had, however, found a bare inch, he whipped out his brand-new pocket-knife and carved his own name over it, and quite felt as if he was adding something to history.

But Bushbo seemed restless. "We can't stay here all day," he said. "This isn't getting us anywhere. We must be off."

"Off where?" rumbled Baobab. "Into the desert, oh Bushlands?"

"Yes, into the desert."

And the great tree shuddered from deepest root to highest branch. But Bushbo did not feel this, for he had rushed out into the open to see if he could get his bearings; and a moment later a sudden cry of wonder from him brought Del out hurrying to his side.

"Look!" said Bushbo, pointing above the far horizon, out across the wide, flat stretch of dry scrubbiness. And there, amongst the few light clouds and gazing straight down at the two boys and Baobab, was a huge face, wrinkled and bearded and the colour of sand. And no matter how long they looked back at it and how much the clouds all around it moved and changed, always the face remained the same, gazing and gazing.

"The spirit of the mighty desert!" whispered Baobab. "And he knows you would threaten him, oh Bushlands."

At which Del felt very much like running back again into Baobab's cool, safe trunk; but not Bushbo.

"No you don't!" he told Del, grabbing his hand and grinning. "I'm sort of responsible for you, you know, and I'm not going to let you out of my sight."

"You're really going, then?" asked Baobab.

"Yes," Bushbo replied. "Upon my sunny word."

"Here then, my fine brave lads," said the tree, snapping off a number of his twigs and branches and throwing them down at the boys' feet. "Take this little gift from your friend Baobab; and when you are so hot and thirsty that you feel you can go no farther, cut open these branches and take out their spongy centres, and squeeze and wring these into your mouths, and you will enjoy a delicious drink."

So the boys gathered up the sticks as fast as they could, and thanked their kind host for all he had done for them, and were preparing to leave him when he called them back.

"Here!" he said, his face wrinkling and twisting and looking uglier than ever with sheer good nature and generosity. "Before you go, drink up this clear, cool water I've stored away in my nooks and hollows."

So Del and Bushbo searched about in all his ruggedness, and soon found what he meant—little woody hollows sheltered from the hot sun and filled with water. With a shout of delight, they set to work and drank from one hollow after another, and then, thanking him once again and each carrying a bundle of his branches, they bade their great, ungainly, hollow, noble-hearted friend good-bye.

CHAPTER V

THE GRASS MAN

OUT they struck towards the east, where the sun rises, and also a little south, heading towards the very heart of this large country which everybody knows about but which only one odd person here and there really understands, and which keeps hidden away inside it some of the oldest and most wonderful secrets in the world. And they had been walking only a very few minutes over the hot sand when they both started back together at the same instant, their eyes popping out to attention with sudden shock, for they had as nearly as anything walked right on top of a man. And there he was now, in spite of his narrow escape, lying out at his full length across the sand, propping himself up on his elbow ever so slightly, and grinning quite unconcernedly.

"A very hearty good day to you, I'm sure!" he rasped out in a voice that was all tangles and stringiness.

And Del, staring at him in silence, and even remembering the wildness of Willie-willie and the broad, gnarled ruggedness of Baobab, thought he had never seen a funnier face. For it looked just like the sound of his voice—tangled and stringy and yellowish-

"A very hearty good day to you, I'm sure!"

brown, with criss-crossing lines all over it; and it was very long, and so thin that it might have been the needle of a pine-tree. And his hair—when Del realized that it *was* his hair, he merely pointed and laughed as if he were at a circus, for it was dull green in colour, and stood up quite straight in one great bundle of spikes.

Bushbo, however, did not see anything particularly funny about him, and immediately returned his jovial greeting. "How good to find *you* here, kind Spinifex!" he said. "With your company our journey won't seem half so long, and not nearly so tiring."

At which Spinifex gave a tremendous stretch, and the longest, narrowest yawn Del had ever seen, and then slowly worked himself up until he was standing on his feet.

Del watched every movement open-mouthed and wide-eyed, and was just thinking there could be no taller man anywhere on earth when—blest if he did not stretch up a little higher. And there he was—every bit of him as thin as his face, and a thick circle of spikes the same colour as his hair hanging down from his waist like a skirt and, at the ends of his absurdly long, yellowish-brown legs, two more circles of spikes round his ankles; and his long, twining toes went spreading out all over the place just like searching roots.

"Of course, you know," he rasped, smiling crookedly, "I'm not at all used to this sort of thing. I feel as right and as graceful as a bandicoot trying to fly, standing up like this. Don't see the sense of it. Lying down is so much better and easier. It's all very well up in the tropics, where there's always tons of water to live on, for grasses to lead a genteel life and go strutting about everywhere on their hind legs; but out here near the desert, I've found that the lower you lie and the more modest your ideas of living, and the less fuss you make of yourself, the better you get along."

"Yes," said Del, gazing thoughtfully all the way up to the top

THE GRASS MAN

of him. "When *you* stand on your hind legs, of course, you make a very big fuss indeed, don't you?"

They all laughed merrily at this, then set out upon their long journey, Spinifex with enormous strides—one to each seven or eight of Del's and Bushbo's—his strong, fibrous toes taking a tight grip of the sand with every step, to steady up his extremely shaky legs.

And although they walked miles and miles like this, drinking from one of old Baobab's branches when they were thirsty and sitting down in the shade of a rock or low shrub when they were particularly hot and tired, their journey did not seem half as long as it really was, and time—day after day of it—flitted past them amongst flocks of white and pink and green and yellow parrots and cockatoos; for that is what time always does when one is happy, and Spinifex was certainly keeping the two boys as happily entertained as they could have wished.

It all started when Del told him that he thought his life must be a frightfully boring one, just lying there all over the hot sands day and night. Then,

"You really think so, do you?" Spinifex had answered. "Well, let me tell you a thing or two about the boring life of an Australian desert grass."

And then he had started telling the most wonderful stories, one after another. First of all he told about his adventures with men and women. "How many times," he said, laughing at the recollection, "have I given the Aboriginal people whole handfuls of my hair and skirt to build their houses with, and their baskets and their fishing nets! And I'll always remember the day when the white men came along. Bossing and bullying individuals they were, and thought they should be given every jolly thing there was; and amongst every jolly thing, of course, were my hair and skirt. Well, I had an argument with them about that." And he grinned widely, relishing the memory. "They went to grab me by the hair—not even bothering to ask, mind you. But I grabbed first—a whole handful—and jabbed it all into them. Yes, yes," he chuckled, "we argued a long time like that. It was great fun. Then at last I gave in, and handed them a fair-sized bundle. After all, I thought, it would be quite interesting to see what they'd do with it when they did get it. And—well, I've never got such a shock in all my life—"

"Why?" Del broke in. "What *did* they do with it?"

"Upon my word, sonny," said Spinifex, running his long, rooty fingers through his bristly hair, "they started making roads with it—and mighty good ones, too."

"Great Scott!" cried Del, and chuckled. "I'd like to see someone trying to make roads out of my hair."

"Oh, I quite got to like the white people after a while," Spinifex continued, "and even gave them some of my gold, as they seemed to think such a lot of it."

"Your gold!" Del repeated, his voice high-pitched. Surely Spinifex was only having a joke with him. This sounded altogether too much like a story of desert-island treasure and adventure. And yet,

"Why, yes, of course," the grass man answered casually. "Nothing so very surprising in that. I've got heaps of gold. And my, how excited people do get when I give them a bit! Any one would think it was as good as a well of water."

"But—but where on earth do you keep it?" Del asked.

"Yes, that's right," Spinifex answered.

"That's right what, you great silly?"

"On the earth, great silly yourself. That's where I keep it. Oh, and under the earth, too, of course."

"But where, where?" Del persisted eagerly. "Here? Just anywhere you happen to be?"

"Well no, not exactly. We—Desert and I—we've got our favourite hoarding places. We used to keep an awful lot over Marble Bar way, and down Coolgardie and Kalgoorlie: but we've given most of it away from there now."

THE GRASS MAN

Del was exasperated. "Where do you keep it now, then?" he asked. "That's what I'm wanting to know."

"No doubt, little friend, no doubt," Spinifex replied, his sharp eyes twinkling. "But I and Desert like our secrets, you know, the same as you boys like yours; and all I'll tell you now is that goodness only knows how long it will be before we'll open our mouths again on the subject of our gold."

And he sounded so definite on this point that Del decided it would be useless to say any more, and walked on in silence. But Spinifex glanced down at him out of the corner of his eye, and seemed mightily amused at his thoughtful face and suddenly, taking his soft hand in his own hard, sinewy one, put something into it.

"Here," he said. "Keep that, little one—just to remember me by."

And Del, looking, saw a rough greyish stone shot through with streaks of shining gold. Full of excitement, he exclaimed about it and wondered at it, and showed it to Bushbo, and held it tightly in his hand for ever so long, then proudly tucked it away in one of his pockets.

Then Spinifex told the boys about his experiences with all kinds of animals and insects—the banquets of golden grain he made a point of providing for hungry sheep, cattle and horses, and—

"Well, look, boys!" he cried out, with a hearty burst of laughter and glancing back over his shoulder. "See for yourselves. I thought they'd be coming along too."

So Del and Bushbo looked round, and what did they see, all crowding along in Spinifex's thin, never-ending shadow, but dozens upon dozens of animals and insects, tiny, little and not so little.

"Trees, mountains and moss-green gullies!" Bushbo exclaimed, and immediately a flock of little blue and brown pigeons came fluttering up and settled all over his hands, arms

MAGIC AUSTRALIA

and shoulders, and hosts of beetles, slower but no less enthusiastic, came trooping after them.

Del clapped his hands with delight, then noticed that Spinifex was having quite a lot to say to a swarm of very thoughtful-looking rabbits and bandicoots who were gazing up at him from amongst his root-like toes, each with its head on one side, and one little front paw held up off the ground.

"No, no," he was saying. "This isn't the time to start burrowing. We're moving on in a minute. You just wait a bit. You'll be sorry if you set your homes up before we've settled."

And behind these was a whole collection of snakes and lizards, sprawling straight out enjoying a rest after their long travels. And at the very back were a few soft, grey kangaroos, with little front paws folded up in a most cuddlesome way, the mothers each carrying one

"No, no. This isn't the time to start burrowing."

THE GRASS MAN

or two woolly babies in her front pocket and the fathers all looking most proud and protective.

"Say, Spinifex," Del asked softly, tugging at one of his skirt spikes, "do they come with you like this wherever you go?"

"Mostly they do," answered Spinifex. "And I don't know what I'd do without them any more than I know what they'd do without me. They're marvellous company for me through the months of loneliness, these little friends of my roots and shadow."

And so it was that, with one thing and another, the hours and days went wheeling by.

But at last one time, round about noon, when the sun was hotter than ever, Del stopped suddenly and pointed towards the horizon; and Bushbo and Spinifex stopped too, and all of them looked alarmed, for there, in the distance, doing their well-known war-dance and dazzling as fire, were the dreaded heat tribes. And the more the three friends watched them the closer did they seem to come, all yelling at the tops of their voices their battle-cry of heat, while the pigeons and beetles fluttered, terrified, between Bushbo and Spinifex, and while all the other little creatures crowded up more closely in Spinifex's narrow strip of shadow, the rabbits and bandicoots trying once more to burrow down amongst his rooty toes.

Then Del, glancing about desperately in every other direction, was the first to catch sight—also in the distance—of something he had almost forgotten existed—a twinkling blue lake, bordered all round with tall reeds as green as emeralds: a place where the savage heat tribes would surely never be able to reach him, let alone do him any harm. "Look!" he cried, grabbing Bushbo and Spinifex each by the hand. "This way!"

But as both his friends only tried to hold him back, he squirmed and struggled until he broke free from them, then ran on alone for all he was worth.

"Stop, little silly!" Spinifex called out after him. "That's nothing—nothing at all. It's something that isn't, I tell you."

But Del took no notice. Spinifex was talking sheer nonsense. That lake was real, all right—marvellously real; indeed it was far more normal than anything that had happened to him since the moment he had first met Bushbo on the edge of that strange cliff way back near Uncle Edward's little house. So on and on he sped, Bushbo and Spinifex making chase behind him, though without any hope of catching him.

But, thought Del after a while, the funny thing was that he could never get any nearer to the sparkling lake. In fact, it almost seemed that the farther towards it he ran the fainter and fainter it grew until at last—no, there could be no mistake about it now. It simply was not there. It had entirely disappeared, leaving him more helpless than ever, with nothing around him except miles and miles of rippling sand—and hordes of savage heat tribes. For indeed, these swarming demons seemed much nearer now than before; and their frantic dancing and threatening battle-cries and fiery breath would have been enough to frighten any small boy just nine years old.

"Oh," cried Del, "what—whatever can we do? Whatever's going to happen to us?"

But Spinifex, who had just caught up with him, only shook him by the shoulders and replied sternly, "Little silly, little silly! Never let me see you following anything like that again. Those are only Desert's dream pictures—mirages—that he dangles in front of people to lead them wild dances far away from water or shade or anything nice and comfortable."

"But—but why?" Del asked impatiently, feeling that none of these queer beings used any common sense at all.

"Why? Because he happens to feel mischievous sometimes, that's why. But remember, Del, that Desert's mischief is dangerous—very dangerous."

"Oh, all right," said Del, wriggling himself free from Spinifex's tight grip and feeling he had been lectured quite long enough. "But what'll we *do*? That's the point. Those s-savage heat tribes—I'll bet you anything they're dangerous too."

Always the face remained the same, gazing and gazing.

MAGIC AUSTRALIA

And now, straining his eyes out into the distance, he suddenly gave a little gasp, and sidled round with the bandicoots and lizards and other creatures into Spinifex's protecting shadow, and made himself as small as he possibly could; for there, gazing down at him again from the now quite clear sky, was that remarkable face—lined, bearded and silent—of the great desert spirit. Only now it seemed a little nearer, perhaps, and also it was smiling. And the longer Del looked at it, the less he liked that smile.

CHAPTER VI

TERRORS AND TEARS

DEL, Bushbo, Spinifex and the animals were entirely trapped, then, and could do nothing, in all those miles upon miles of flatness and barrenness, to escape from the vicious heat tribes who were swarming up around them from every direction —all dazzling white and golden in colour–and who were now near enough to open fire upon them. And open fire they did. Dancing, yelling and making all kinds of weird-looking faces, those millions of tiny imps suddenly took aim, all of them at the same moment, and shot out a storm of little white-hot arrows.

Del clung on to Spinifex's spindly legs as tightly as he could, and pressed himself against them; but nothing was any use. Those horrid little arrows found him wherever he was, and soon he was stung all over, and drops of perspiration were trickling out from every wound, making him feel more frightened and uncomfortable than he remembered ever having been before. And he kept wondering and wondering what would happen to him next, and if the savage imps really meant to finish him off altogether.

Bushbo, however, was very brave, and stood up straight, facing them. After all, this was one of the things he had come for —an interview with these lawless tribes—and he meant to make the most of it.

"Silence! Silence!" he shouted, above their deafening din.

But they only yelled the louder and danced the more wildly.

"Savage, vengeful little creatures, will you never learn kindness and peace?" he continued.

MAGIC AUSTRALIA

But their only reply to this was to come jostling and elbow-pushing their way up so close as almost to stifle him. Then, joining hands in ring after ring, they went tearing around him madly, so quickly that Del could hardly see where one of them

Bushbo, however, was very brave.

ended and the next began; and besides, every time he tried to look his eyes got stung, so he simply shut them and listened, and this was what he heard—the heat imps' battle-cry, yelled out fiercely by all of them together, as they danced round Bushbo:

> "We'll prick him and kick him
> And arrow him through,
> And pelt him and melt him
> To boiling hot brew.
> Or lop him and chop him
> For potsful of stew!"

"How terrible!" Del thought. "Poor Bushbo! Whatever can we do for him?" And all sorts of bold, clever and heroic ideas

TERRORS AND TEARS

came dashing into his mind, but—poor Del—as soon as he opened his eyes and looked at those hosts of prancing savages, he did not feel the least bit brave any longer.

So altogether, things were looking very bad indeed, and the more Bushbo tried to talk the less he could manage to make himself even heard, and Del, Spinifex and the animals were all extremely worried about him. But as it happened, Desert was not to have everything his own way, and the heat tribes were not to be the only ones dancing over the barrenness; for suddenly, shadows ever so much larger than Spinifex's began to appear all over the ground, and, looking up, the travellers saw great fleets of clouds flying out across the sky—flying so quickly and in such dark swarms that Del was sure he could hear them zooming thunderously.

And the wonderful part about it was that the savages, also glancing up, began to fidget and look uncomfortable and murmur something about a hasty retreat. And, as soon as they left the way clear for him, Bushbo came over and stood beside Del, putting one arm around his shoulders. "Poor old chap!" he said, beaming. "You didn't bargain for anything like this, did you?"

And Del had to admit that he hadn't.

Meanwhile Spinifex, shading his eyes, had been examining the cloud fleets in silence, and now murmured doubtfully, "I wonder if they really are passenger clouds? Seems almost too good to be true."

Del glanced up at Bushbo inquiringly.

"He means he wonders if they're carrying the rain sprites," Bushbo explained.

"Wonders!" Del repeated. "Why, he must be mad. Of course they're carrying rain. What would they be so black for if they weren't?"

And indeed, neither Bushbo nor Spinifex had time to answer him back when down came, shooting, diving and plunging, crowds upon crowds of tiny silvery sprites. And the last straggling little heat savages, as soon as they saw the rain sprites, stood still in utter amazement, then abruptly turned on their heels and scampered off for all they were worth.

And now the air, instead of being filled with harsh, fierce battle-cries, rang merrily with millions of tiny tinkling bells; for that was what the laughter of the rain sprites sounded like.

And Del, watching closely, noticed something else that he simply must remember to tell Uncle Edward about when he got home again. Each of the wee sprites, after landing and turning a few somersaults and catherine-wheels, rushed to and fro everywhere, knocking on the ground in as many places as they possibly could. Then, after a very little while, each of these places opened up like a little door, and out popped a bright, smiling flower or a tuft of soft, shy grass. So no wonder was it that, search as he might, Del could no longer see anything of Desert anywhere, for what had been only dry sand and a bit of prickly grass a very short while ago was now a forest of wild flowers.

It was certainly one of the prettiest sights Del had ever seen. But just as he was feeling happiest about it, something went wrong. Suddenly there was no more rain and the fleet of clouds had vanished, and Del noticed that the silvery sprites, standing tiptoed and shimmering everywhere, on the pointy tips of grass

Up sprang the sand imps, like streaks of dusty lightning.

TERRORS AND TEARS

blades and flower petals, began glancing about in a nervous and worried manner, almost as if they expected something awful to happen any minute. And he had scarcely any time to wonder what this strange something might be when, with a great shout of glee, up sprang simply millions of grubby-faced little sand imps, who pounced upon the rain sprites like streaks of dusty lightning and, in the twinkling of an eye, binding them hand and foot, had pushed and pulled and bullied them down, down, down, far into the darkness under the earth. And everything was dry and thirsty-looking again.

Del was so disappointed that all of a sudden he felt too tired to walk another step; so he sat down right where he was, determined to stop there and be miserable for the next five days. And Bushbo and Spinifex also seemed tired, for they sat down too, one on either side of him. But, try as they might, they could not stay miserable long, for Spinifex started going back over the years again and remembering wonderful stories; and Bushbo, also, had plenty to tell, about the many birds, plants and animals that came and lived happily with him although they refused to live in any other part of the world.

Then, gradually, they stopped talking and merely sat thinking. And everything else seemed to sit thinking too, for there was silence everywhere—a lovely, peaceful silence. After a while, however, Del thought he heard something, and he listened intently, and got Bushbo and Spinifex to listen too, and —yes—they all thought they heard something. Very soft it was, to be sure; but each of them, being a gallant gentleman, felt he simply must do something about it, for what they heard was a silvery, bubbly sobbing, which seemed to be coming from somewhere under the ground.

"Could—could it be the rain sprites?" Del whispered.

"We'll soon find out, that's one thing certain," Spinifex replied, doubling himself up and getting his rooty toes and fingers all to work on the same spot, wriggling their way down into the earth as far as they could go.

MAGIC AUSTRALIA

And now the rabbits and bandicoots grew very excited, for if Spinifex was burrowing, they felt they had an excellent excuse for burrowing too; so they did burrow, with all their might. And Del and Bushbo, who could not possibly be left out, also got down on their hands and knees, and scraped and dug as they never had before.

Every little while they all stopped and listened, to make sure they were going in the right direction; and there could be no doubt about it, the farther down they went the more clearly they could hear that sad, silvery sobbing. Yet, work as they might, and ever so deep as their hole was quickly growing, it seemed that they would never come to anything except earth and more earth.

"Dear me!" said Del, brushing his hair up off his eyes. "This is terrible. Those sprites are so tiny that, if they're not careful, they'll drown themselves before we can get to them, they're crying so much—the sillies!" And, setting to work again, he dug faster than ever.

At last, when they were all so far down that even the daylight could scarcely find its way through to them, they suddenly came to a rocky shelf and, quickly jostling on to it together, they all leaned over as far as they could and peered down.

It was some time before they could see anything because of the darkness; but when at last they could, there, sitting with her hands over her eyes and her lovely sparkling hair falling around her like a long cape, was a graceful lady silvery white and almost transparent.

Del caught his breath in silent wonder, but Spinifex merely stood and looked on as if he were not in the least surprised, and Bushbo called softly, "Hail, lovely spirit! What troubles you?"

"Ah," she replied, also very softly, looking up, her eyes shining with tears, "you lucky, lucky beings who live up there in the golden light of day! I am troubled because I have been a prisoner here for hundreds of years, and because the sand imps have just captured millions more of my tiny sprites and brought them down here to live with me in darkness for ever and ever."

TERRORS AND TEARS

"*Your* sprites!" said Del, wide-eyed. "But—but who are you, then?" he asked a little lamely.

"I am Water," she answered, smiling through her tears, "sent down from heaven to refresh the earth and make things grow. But alas, how can I do this when Desert is so cruel a tyrant, and his sand tribes are so strong and keep me buried here so deeply, where the roots of thirsty plants can never reach me?"

"I have been a prisoner here for hundreds of years."

At which Spinifex nodded, grunting his ardent approval.

Del slowly scratched his head. It was indeed a difficult problem. "But surely there's something we could do about it," he said, "some way we could get you out of there—"

"I too am the friend of living things," Bushbo interrupted eagerly, "and that is why I have come here—to reason with the heat and sand tribes and—"

"Ah," the beautiful lady broke in, shaking her head and

sighing, "why waste time with them, kind helper? They will never listen to a word you say.

And Del was just about to say something when suddenly there was a movement from every side at once of the deep hole he had helped to dig and, before any of them could even guess what was happening, thousands of indignant sand imps had rushed in upon them and done their best to knock them senseless, much to their amazement and confusion.

"Oh," cried the silver lady, flinging her arms up towards her kind friends, "hurry, hurry! For my sake. Don't let the sand imps bury you, for if they do, you'll never escape, and I shall have no one to plead for me."

So hurry they did. Climbing and scrambling, grunting and puffing, Del, Bushbo, Spinifex and the animals hurried for all they were worth up towards the top again, the sand imps doing everything possible to trip them by slithering under their feet and to blind them by flying straight into their eyes. And when at last they did manage to tumble out into the daylight again, they were so exhausted that they could do nothing for ever so long except lie sprawled out panting and groaning—lizards, beetles and all.

But the lovely water spirit could only stay where she was —deep, deep down under the ground.

CHAPTER VII

THE GREEN GIANT

ONE morning not long after this, Del awoke earlier than usual, and as soon as he did he sat bolt upright and stared, then rubbed his eyes hard, and squeezed and blinked them; but nothing made any difference. He still saw what he had seen to begin with—an enormous green face with scrubby hair and eyebrows, and sparkling beryl eyes with smile wrinkles at their corners. And once again he wondered what on earth could have happened to him in his sleep, or if, perhaps, he was only imagining things now.

Without breathing a word, he glanced down at Bushbo and Spinifex, still fast asleep beside him, then quickly looked back again, almost expecting to find that it—whatever it was—had vanished. But no, it had not vanished.

That being the case, he next, ever so gingerly and not daring to stand up, leaned across, stretched his neck out as far as it would go, and peeped over to see if he really was—as he seemed to be—sitting on the edge of something yards and yards above the flat ground he had been used to for so long. And then immediately he jerked back with a terrific start, for—sure enough—he was.

Suddenly, at that, there came a soft rumble of laughter, which grew louder and louder until Del thought it must be cracking his ears. Bushbo and Spinifex sprang up, wide awake and full of questions, but Del only screwed shut his eyes and pressed his fingers into his ears; and he was just deciding that he really must try to be brave about whatever it was that was surely going to happen to him now when the laughter stopped, and he heard Bushbo's familiar voice, not in the least disturbed, call out:

"Hail, Macdonnell Ranges! Though we travelled on last night into the darkness and lay down to sleep we knew not where, I had no idea we could have come as far as this."

Whereupon Macdonnell Ranges laughed again—a long, deep-voiced laugh—and Del stared up at him gravely, though still distrustfully.

"Oh, come now, little chappie!" said the enormous green face. "Don't look at me like that. I'm your friend, don't you know!" Then, turning to Bushbo, he continued, "As for your remark, my dear boy from the east, you are quite right. You, indeed, had not come as far as this—not by a long way. But have you never heard of the wonderful spell I hold, lying here in the middle of the desert with my grasses and trees and coolness and little water wells? Have you never heard how desert travellers are drawn to me from ever so far away? Well, I really did do it this time," he declared, with another rumble of laughter. "I drew you to me while you slept. And upon my word, holding you here so still on the tips of my fingers all this time, I thought you'd never wake up."

Like a flash Del sprang to his feet. "On the tips of your fingers!" he exclaimed, and got such a shock that he lost his balance and fell, rolling and bounding down the slope as if he were a little round pebble. Whereupon Bushbo, Spinifex and the animals went scuttling after him—for the sheer joy of it.

"Oh my heavens!" Del cried out when he came to a stop at last and found himself deep down in one of the loveliest valleys imaginable, green with delicious grass and ferns, gumtrees, and the straightest, tallest palms he had ever seen; and, what was more, with a real creek dimpling its way right through it and twinkling in the sunlight.

"Oh, but my goodness, what palms!" Del exclaimed, having to swing his head back as far as it would go so as to see the tufty topknots of the tallest ones. "Well," chuckled the voice of the ranges, "what would you expect? You awoke on the tips of my cupped-up fingers, as you know; and then sent yourself spinning down into—well, into my Palm Valley, don't you see!"

Held in the Palm Valley of a green giant's hand.

"Heavens, yes! Of course," said Del. "I might have guessed that."

"And," Bushbo panted excitedly, out of breath but in very high spirits, "you're mightily proud of your palm treasures, aren't you, O Ranges?"

"Naturally," came the prompt reply, as the rugged green face, glancing down at them from way up, wrinkled itself with smiles more deeply than ever. "And," he added, "wouldn't you be, too, if they were yours and you knew that there weren't any others the same in the whole world?"

"My word, yes!" Del replied fervently, in a voice that sounded as if it might have come from an ant after the ranges's thundering tones. "But look, what's Desert got to say about your having them? Doesn't he get wild?"

"Ho-ho-ho!" answered the ranges. "That's a good one, to be sure—'What's Desert got to say'! Why, he's got nothing to say, of course—nothing that counts, that is. No doubt he mumbles away to himself no end about them, but he can't do anything else. He can bully things about right up to where I begin, and start again exactly where I end, but—ho-ho-ho!—I'd like to see him trying to lord it over me—the nasty-natured old stick-in-the-sand!"

Well, it was odd—very odd—thought Del, being held like this in the Palm Valley of a green giant's hand, with the giant himself gazing down on to him. And he started to wander about exploring things—wading in the creek, scaling over rocks, peering into the centres of fern clumps, climbing a gum-tree, and then fiddling about up the rocky and grassy slopes. Yes, it was very odd indeed; but great fun too—particularly now, when he began finding things amongst the grass; any amount of sparkling little pebbles, green, white, red. Gurgling with delight, he picked up a few of these and turned them over and over in his hand, and was just about to ask something about them when the most upsetting thing happened. He was snatched up off his feet, whirled away over what seemed a tremendous distance, then held suspended in mid air by the tops of his trousers, kicking, squirming and screaming for all he was worth.

At last, exhausted and terribly frightened, he stopped, and hung there quite still. And then for the first time he heard

THE GREEN GIANT

Bushbo's and Spinifex's laughter echoing over to him from far away, through mountains and gullies; and also the rippling peal of a bell-bird, while a family of bower-birds, having listened intently for some time to this medley of sound, suddenly all struck out together, imitating everything at once—Bushbo, Spinifex, rivers, bell-bird, rustling palms and gum-trees—until the whole air throbbed with chuckles and laughter.

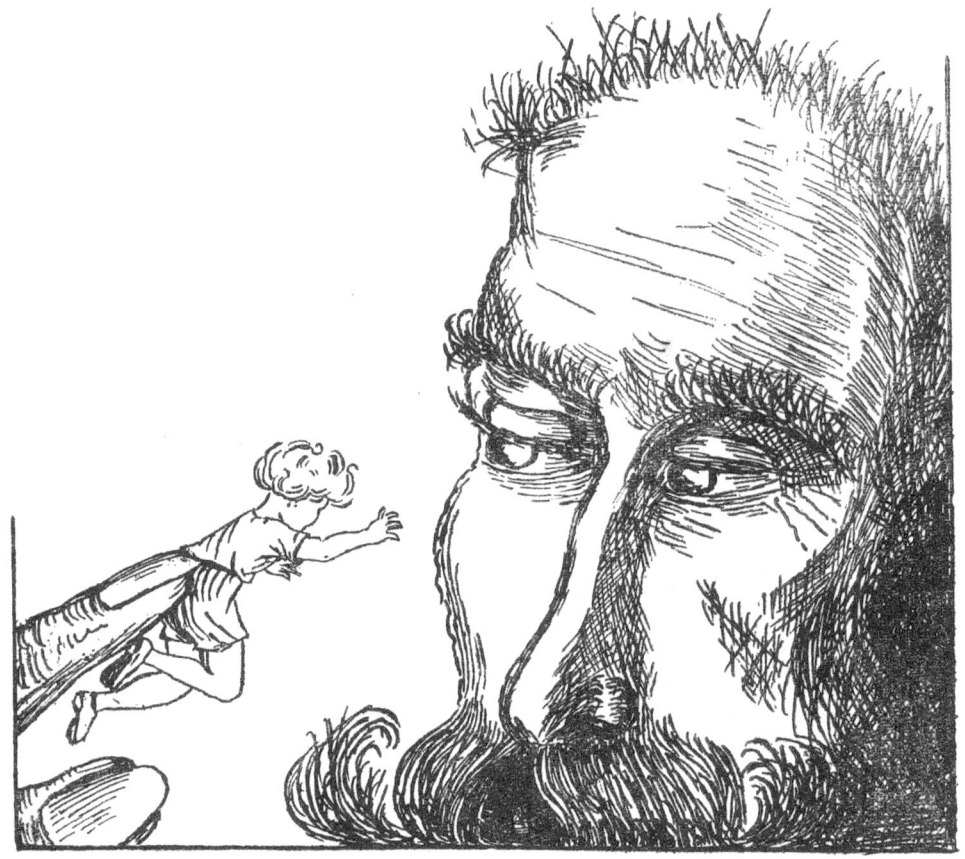

"What were you doing with my jewels?"

It would have been quite nice in a way, only Del hated to be laughed at, and he was certain it was he they were laughing at; he hated to be made look silly, and he knew he must be looking extremely silly. And altogether, he was growing less and less frightened and more and more indignant when he caught sight of Macdonnell Ranges's huge, merry green eyes, right there only a few inches away from him—and that, finally, was more than he could stand.

"I say, look here, every one," he shouted, his face red with anger, "you—you just can't treat me like this, I tell you. I—I won't have it. A chap doesn't know where he stands for two minutes with all you—you—whatever you are. I'm not being treated right, I tell you—not right at all. I'm no baby. I'm nine."

And he tried to stamp his foot, but of course he could do nothing of the sort, and Bushbo, Spinifex and Macdonnell Ranges laughed longer and louder than ever.

Then, "What were you doing with my jewels," thundered the voice of the ranges, trying to sound annoyed, "my crystal, my beryls, my rubies? That's what I want to know."

"Oh, bother your crystal and beryls and rubies!" Del retorted, looking like a stormy hen. "You've made me drop them now, anyway. Goodness knows where they are—and it's your fault, not mine."

"Well, well, well, I s'pose I'll have to forgive you this time," said the green giant, his voice kind and soothing.

"And—and while you're about it," Del added, frowning, "I do wish you'd put me down. I'm sick of this."

"All right, laddie, all right!" And the green face wrinkled up until there seemed to be little smiling creeks running all over it, and Del found himself beginning to like the fellow in spite of everything.

Another quick whisk through the air, and he was deposited once more deep down in the safe and cosy Palm Valley of the giant's other hand. And there he was treated to such a hearty welcome by Bushbo and Spinifex that he soon forgot all his grievances and became a very amiable little boy indeed.

"And now," said Macdonnell Ranges, "before you boys go on —as I know you are going—into the land of ghosts and

THE GREEN GIANT

memories that lies between me and my brother Flinders Range, I must give you a little something to eat and drink—"

"Land of ghosts!" cried Del. "That sounds awful. *I'm* not going there, that's one thing certain. I'm staying here. You're not a bit a bad sort, you know," he added generously, thrusting his hands into his pockets and gazing up into the huge, kindly face.

"Oh yes you are," said Bushbo—"going into the ghost and memory land, I mean; for I'm going, and I've told you I'm not letting you out of my sight."

"I'm not going!" Del repeated, stamping his foot really hard this time, to make up for when he had not been able to at all.

But Bushbo only smiled at him in a sure, grown-up way, and murmured, "You'll see!"

And Del said no more about it, for he knew deep inside him that he would not part with Bushbo for anything in the world, no matter how many ghost lands they might have to face together. And besides, Del told himself, holding his head up high and looking superior, he was no coward; he was a boy of nine, and he had a brand-new pocket-knife; and if these silly creatures thought they could make him believe in ghosts, he would soon show them how mistaken they were.

So, after eating as many wild berries as they liked, handed over to them by their giant green friend, and after Spinifex, particularly, had drunk cool water to his heart's content, Bushbo announced that they must be off, and Del murmured under his breath that he supposed he would be going along too.

But Spinifex cocked his head on one side and stayed sitting down, thinking deeply. Then, "Look here, you two," he said, twiddling his toes down into the earth that Macdonnell Ranges held, and sprawling out until he looked much the same as he had when Del and Bushbo had first met him, "I don't think I'll go any farther, you know that? As far as I can reckon, this is a perfect life here, with all sorts of slopes and valleys to wander over, and—well, I just feel as if I'd like to stay put, if you understand."

"Yes, you good old thing, of course we understand," said Bushbo.

Macdonnell Ranges listened to every word with a twinkle in his eye.

"So it's really good-bye, then?" Del asked, casually twirling one of the green bristles standing straight up from Spinifex's head.

"Well, until we meet again some time, little one," the raspy, stringy, pointy grass man replied.

Then they began to feel themselves being gently lowered —down, down, down from the cool heights into the warm plains once more. But the many animals, who spent their lives following Spinifex's shadow, were now too happy at the idea of a long, peaceful spell to bother about feeling anything else.

"Well I never! Look at those rabbits and bandicoots!" said Del, laughing. "They're not wasting much time, are they?"

But when Bushbo looked, there was nothing to be seen except dozens of freshly dug burrows, all in amongst Spinifex's twisted, rooty toes.

At last the coming down stopped. The huge green hand, earthy, bushy, ferny and grassy, rested flat on the sands, and Del and Bushbo got themselves off it with a run and a jump.

"Thank you, dear old Macdonnell Ranges!" Bushbo cried out, waving up towards the great scrubby head which was now bent, looking down at them.

"Yes, thank you for everything!" Del shouted.

"It's been a treat to have you," thundered the giant's voice, "even for so short a time. And you, little one, you've quite forgiven me?"

" 'Course!" Del replied, looking down and grinning sheepishly.

"Then hold out your hands, little friend, and let me see if I can give you something to take home and remember me by."

So Del obeyed, his heart pirouetting with excitement, and immediately Macdonnell Ranges's other hand came swinging over and, into the little cup Del had formed, dropped a tinkling

He looked just like a great, purple range of mountains.

twinkling shower of coloured pebbles, red, green and white; and lastly, a little squarish block of something which would peel off into an endless number of thin, smokily transparent leaves, like the pages of a book.

"Oh, thank you, thank you, dear Ranges!" Del shouted. "They're wonderful. I'll keep them always."

"In case you don't know," said the giant, "that little square is one of my books of mica—pocket edition," he added with a wink.

"Pocket edition indeed!" Bushbo declared. "You should just see some of the huge volumes he has in his mica library, Del, for that's one of his favourite minerals, isn't it, O Ranges? And he keeps simply thousands of books of it, all sealed away in strong rock cases."

"That sounds great!" Del remarked.

And then, with a final good-bye, the two boys left him. But for ever so long afterwards they kept turning and waving to their friend the rugged green giant who lay reclined there against the sky—massive, cool, and very very generous; until at last, looking back, they could scarcely distinguish head from knees or hands from shoulders, for, in the waning light, he looked just like a great, purple range of mountains.

CHAPTER VIII

THE LITTLE RED DESERT PEA OF MEMORY LAND

AFTER the shade and coolness with Macdonnell Ranges, Del thought the desert worse than ever. And it was, to be sure, worse than anything he and Bushbo had yet travelled through, for never had either of them seen such an endless waste of sand, and of little rounded stones or gibbers that made walking very hard and uncomfortable. And not only this, but the sand was so piercingly white that it shimmered in the sunlight just as if it were still the laughing, flowing water of the ranges instead of merely the bone-dry bed of a great river that used to run there in the long, long ago. Lovely sparkling waters all around him, thought Del, and none of them anything but make-believe—none of them anything but white sand and little round stones. So that at last he got very tired and grumpy, and made such a noise about it that Bushbo grew a trifle short-tempered too.

"Can't say I'm having much of a joy trip myself, old chap," he retorted. "And with you going on like that, it's only about a dozen times worse than it might be. Remember, I didn't ask you to come. I told you to start with that you probably wouldn't like it. So now, if you don't, the least you could do would be to keep quiet about it."

"Oh, all right," said Del, and thrust his hands into his pockets, deciding not to say another word about anything. That would make Bushbo sorry, he thought.

However, they had not gone far like this when, a little ahead of them, they saw, peeping up over a shallow sandy bank, something that made them both stop and wonder. Then, immediately afterwards, Bushbo gave a short, joyous laugh and ran towards it,

Del following him closely; for this particular something had been two little jet-black feet, crossed at the ankles, and, a bit farther along, the tip of a pointed red cap.

"Hail, Desert Pea!" cried Bushbo, running.

And when he and Del came to a standstill on the edge of the low embankment, there, gazing up at them and beaming merrily, was a dear little jet-black face, with a longish narrow body all dressed in red lying tummy-downwards between it and the little black feet.

"Hail, Bush from the east—and little one!" he added gaily.

"What might you be doing in this land of ghosts and memories? If you're going farther on, I should like to bear you company."

"This," said Bushbo, taking Del's hand, "is my young mortal friend. Shockingly bad-tempered he is, but a splendid pal just the same. As for me, I'm searching for some spot, through all this sad barrenness, where Desert might be persuaded to let my trees and flowers and other creatures live."

"By the red of my cap and the black of my toes," Desert Pea exclaimed, "you'll find no such spot around here. True, the rain sprites do their best from time to time, and knock up a few other flowers beside myself, but old Desert's too strong for them."

"As far as I can see," Del remarked, "it's mighty hard for anything to live out here; I haven't seen any people, either."

"Oh, some people do get interested in a few things now and then," said the little red desert pea, blinking. "They come out hunting dingoes quite often, and chasing after Opal and lots of other gems that happen to be lying about here. But they never stay very long. Something always seems to dishearten them."

"What sort of something?" Del asked.

"Oh, droughts, or dust-storms, or even floods, or the playfulness of what he's looking for. Things out here are often playful, you know—particularly Opal—and lead mortals the wildest dances you could think of."

"Hail, Desert Pea!"

MAGIC AUSTRALIA

"I see," said Del. But he looked rather doubtful just the same.

"Well," Bushbo declared, "we're going to try our luck, anyway. So if you'd really care to come with us, Desert Pea, it would be awfully good to have you."

"Of course I'll care to come," cried the little fellow, springing to his feet and streaking and zigzagging all over the place just to show how much ground he could cover and how energetic he was.

So Del, Bushbo and Desert Pea travelled on together for some time. Then suddenly Del stopped, frowning stormily, and burst out, "Look here, you chaps, this is a take-in, that's what I call it. Land of ghosts and memories be bothered! I've been looking everywhere for a ghost for hours, since every one's talked such an awful lot about them, and of course—just as I could have told you ages ago—I haven't as much as seen a sign of one. And as for memories—well, I've been remembering Uncle Edward and things; but I can remember them just as well anywhere else. And —and it's all the biggest take-in I ever knew, I tell you."

"But," Desert Pea protested, sprinting up and peeping out at him mischievously from under his cap, "you don't seem to understand. Australia herself—the whole of her—has the oldest memory in all the world."

"Well, but how?" Del asked impatiently. "And why? And what sort of things does she remember?"

"Why? Simply because she's been living above the sea far longer than any other country there is," said Bushbo. "And beyond that we can't tell you anything just yet, old chap. We can't tell the very first reasons—the most important ones."

"Oh bother!" Del exploded. "Why not? What's the jolly idea?"

"Because we, her native creatures—her animals and forests and plains and caves and mountains—we have all promised her solemnly not to tell the secret of her ancient life to any man."

Del frowned. "Not even to me, though?"

Bushbo and the little red desert pea both shook their heads sadly.

THE LITTLE RED DESERT PEA OF MEMORY LAND

"Not even to you," Bushbo repeated.

Anyway, Del thought, strutting on, what did he care? He had a brand-new pocket-knife, didn't he? And Spinifex had given him a piece of gold, and Macdonnell Ranges a handful of jewels and a book of mica. What else could a young man of nine desire?

But suddenly Desert Pea grabbed Del's arm and pointed into the distance. "Look!" he cried excitedly. "Look, Del! One of the memories!"

"One of the ghosts!" Bushbo added.

But Del, straining and blinking and staring, could see absolutely nothing for some time. "Oh, you're only kidding!" he declared. "You think you can tell me any jolly thing you like. Well—"Then, all in a moment, he did see what they meant, and stood quite still with a little gulp.

Far, far away something was moving, like a great human mist. It was the palest possible blue in colour, and reared up to a head of sparkling white, and the whole of it, as it slid gracefully forward as proudly as an ancient galleon, shone softly in the sunlight.

"Say, wh-what'll we do?" cried Del, turning slightly pale. "The—the jolly thing's coming up this way."

" 'Twon't bite you," said Desert Pea, grinning.

"No, of course not," Bushbo assured him. "Ghosts aren't real things any longer—just memories of what used to be. They can't hurt any one."

"Great Scott, I know that!" Del exclaimed, holding his head up high and looking indignant. "But," he added after a while, still watching the mist suspiciously, "how do you know it isn't one of those things that aren't at all—like the lake? Remember? What's the difference?"

"There's a very big difference," said Bushbo. "Mirages—the things that aren't—look like things that really do exist somewhere or other, even if hundreds of miles away. But ghosts, I tell you, are memories of things that were once and aren't now. So you see," and he placed his hand on Del's shoulder, "there's nothing at all to worry about, old chap."

"I know that!" Del cried out, shaking Bushbo off, then looking back at the pale blue, shining mist out of the corner of his eye.

On and on it came—nearer and nearer—rolling, rearing, gliding. But no matter what it did, neither Bushbo nor Desert Pea took any notice; and when, covering the whole of everything as it came, it was almost on top of them, Del could stand it no longer.

On and on it came—nearer and nearer.

THE LITTLE RED DESERT PEA OF MEMORY LAND

"But I say, really," he burst out at last, "wh-what are we going to do about it?"

"Nothing, of course," said the little red desert pea. "Just let it pass over us, then go on the same as ever. It often comes gliding about like this. I'm quite used to it," he added proudly, folding his jet-black arms in front of him, and smiling all over his jet-black face.

And hardly had he finished speaking when the great ghost was upon them—rolling over them as if it had no idea of their existence. And Del noticed that it had something like long, trailing-sleeved arms spread straight out on either side of it, and that its white face looked sad; but he saw nothing more, for he had suddenly ducked his head in against Bushbo's arm and had closed his eyes as tightly as he could. And when after a moment, not feeling anything, he peeped up gingerly, he found that the strange spirit had gone and was nowhere to be seen, and that Bushbo and Desert Pea were grinning broadly at him.

Del strutted away a step or two and kicked up a bit of sand. "What was it, anyway?" he asked.

"The ghost of the sea," answered the little red desert pea. "The sea that used to wash over these sands goodness knows how many thousands of years ago."

"Glory!" Del murmured under his breath. And the three of them walked on a little farther.

Only a very little farther, though, Del suddenly pounced on something gleaming up at him from the crevice of a rock like a scrap of sunset shot through with emerald and lightning. When he saw it first he had no idea of what it might be, yet somehow or other he felt that unless he were very quick it would dart away from him, high up into the sky or deep down under the ground. So, when he actually had caught it, he quite crowed with delight, while Bushbo and Desert Pea only laughed at him. "By the tip of my ebony nose!" Desert Pea exclaimed merrily. "There really wasn't much hurry, Del. That's been lying there for the last few thousand years."

"What?" Del squeaked.

"Don't you see?" Bushbo explained. "That's just another memory—only of a different kind."

"No," said Del, "I don't see at all. How? Memory of what?"

"Once upon a time," said the little red desert pea, beaming, "long before men and women had learnt how to read and write, there was a wee cockle-shell fish who was so proud of his home that he wished and wished something could be done to make it last for ever. Mother Sea, when she found this out, was extremely amused, and teased the wee fish no end for his vanity, and all his brother and sister fish teased him too. Still, in spite of everything, he kept on feeling the same about it, and at last along came Opal, and breathed her spell over his pretty house. And so, there it is to-day, its shape exactly the same as ever, only covered with a coat of many-coloured fire." And, laughing, Desert Pea sprinted ahead so quickly, zigzagging all over the ground like a bright red flame, that for a while Del could scarcely see where he was and where he wasn't.

"Heavens!" he murmured seriously. Then, "Say, Bushbo, do you think it would be all right for me to take this—this memory home with me?"

And Bushbo, glancing at the curled opally shell lying there in the palm of Del's hand and, after all those centuries, still looking strangely alive, told him he was sure it would be quite all right.

So Del kept holding it tightly for a long time in his hot, grubby hand, then popped it into his pocket with all the other things.

Suddenly Desert Pea came rushing back as if he were being chased by something, but Del and Bushbo soon found that, as usual, he was only laughing. When he got right up to them he turned and whistled.

"What's that for?" Del asked.

But before Desert Pea could answer him, there came flashing up over a little rise a great, handsome yellow dog.

THE LITTLE RED DESERT PEA OF MEMORY LAND

Del was delighted, for he loved dogs, and "Oh," he cried, stooping down, "what a bonzer chap! Here, boy! Here!"

But the dingo's only answer was to cast him a wicked, unfriendly glance.

Desert Pea giggled, stroking the soft, yellow head. "No, *you'd* better not touch him, Del," he warned. "He's quite wild, you know, and doesn't like mortals. Every other kind of dog all over

A great, handsome yellow dog.

the world is more or less brought up by men—all except this fellow."

Del frowned. "Oh, I don't care, anyway," he muttered.

And he muttered even more when the lovely animal, noticing Bushbo, bounded up and sniffed around him in an affectionate manner.

"Poor old dingo!" said Bushbo, stroking him and laughing. "He gets a pretty bad time of it, don't you, boy? Just about as bad a time as he gives."

"How?" Del asked curtly.

"Well, you see, Dingo eats grasshoppers in the Desert but men think that he hunts sheep and kills them, so men hunt him and kill him. And it's an awful shame that they don't behave better, for—well, he's one of the memories, really; again in a different way."

"What?" cried Del. "Oh, but how can he be?"

"Simply by going back and back goodness knows how long—most likely farther back than the very first men and women. Other dogs have changed entirely since then, and got all sorts of fancy ideas into their heads and forgotten nearly everything about their ancestors. But this fellow's never forgotten, and he's never changed. In fact, for all any one could tell, without knowing, he's just one of his own ancestors come to life."

The great yellow dog looked from Bushbo to Desert Pea and blinked lovingly, but when he came to Del he bared a few of his teeth and an evil glint flashed into his eyes—which made Del creep a lot nearer to Bushbo than he had wanted to—then suddenly he turned and prowled away over the sands that were so much the same colour as himself.

"Well I never!" said Del. "Like one of his own ancestors come to life, eh? I'll have to tell Uncle Edward about that."

"Yes," Desert Pea brought in airily, "animals in Australia just don't forget. That's one of the special things about them. To-day, other countries only have drawings and a few odd bones of those huge brutes with strong, dragging tails that used to prowl about before history started being written, but Australia has the real live kangaroo—much smaller than the ancient chaps, of course, and nicer mannered, but one of them just the same.

"What about the good old platypus, who lives in my creeks and rivers?" Bushbo quickly brought in. "By this time, animals in other countries have quite decided what they want to be, and have settled down to be it and nothing else—bird, fish, or furry land-dweller. But no, not the platypus. After all these hundreds

THE LITTLE RED DESERT PEA OF MEMORY LAND

and thousands of years he still hasn't made up his mind nor quite forgotten how to be any one of them, so he hasn't even started straightening himself out yet."

"Straightening himself out?" Del repeated, looking puzzled, and getting a picture of Uncle Edward hammering bent nails into shape.

"Yes," Bushbo explained, "into one thing or another. So that, you see, he still wears a fur coat like a bear's, yet hangs on to his webbed feet and swims like a frog, and Mrs Platypus lays eggs like a bird, and then feeds her children on milk like a cow or a dog or a camel—"

"Great Scott!" Del burst in. "I wish I could see one. I never have, you know. Do you think you could give me a little platypus for a pet, Bushbo?"

But Bushbo only laughed. "I'm afraid not," he said. "You see, platypuses are shy creatures, and they depend on me to hide and protect them. They'd feel very hurt about it if I handed one of them over to a mortal boy."

"Oh bother!" Del retorted, scowling. "It strikes me you people won't do a single thing for us mortals, and it isn't fair. You're—you're mean, that's what you are."

But the little red desert pea again peeped up at him from under his cap, his eyes twinkling. "When mortals learn kindness, Del, we'll do anything we can for them, and give them everything we've got."

"Sh!" Bushbo suddenly commanded, grabbing Del's arm and pointing up into the sky.

"Oh yes," Desert Pea whispered, jumping with excitement, "take a good look at that, Del, for it's another memory. It's as old as old can be. Other countries have forgotten all about it by now, for it's so long since they saw it; and even Australia doesn't seem to remember it more than once in a human lifetime these days. A wonderful old bird, that—a special kind of parrot."

"Heavens!" cried Del. "I reckon I am fairly lucky after all."

MAGIC AUSTRALIA

And he strained his eyes up towards the white, fluffy clouds. But the only thing he could see was a little spot of scarlet flying silently and quickly—all too quickly—farther and farther away from him.

"That's the scarlet of his crest," said Bushbo.

Then Desert Pea gave a funny zigzagging chuckle, and proudly waggled the tip of his cap. "I've got a red crest too!" he chanted. "I've got a red crest too!"

CHAPTER IX

CAUGHT!

THE next morning Del, Bushbo and Desert Pea woke up suddenly at the same moment, with a mysterious frothy sound bubbling in their ears.

"Whatever is it?" Del whispered, peering through the misty light.

But Bushbo and the little red desert pea looked at each other and nodded, smiling. Although they could not be quite sure what it was, they had a very good idea, and they were just about to do a bit of stretching and yawning before grabbing Del and rushing out of danger when, with a great frothy shout, a grey, goggle-eyed, dragon-looking creature reared up over a sandy rise right behind them and came crashing down on top of them with all the enthusiasm of an overgrown puppy.

Then followed a dreadful moment, when nobody knew anything about what was happening to himself or any one else, and when all three of them choked and gurgled and gulped and spluttered, and flapped their arms and legs about in all kinds of extraordinary antics, bumping and kicking themselves and each other without having the slightest idea of what they were really doing. At last, however, one by one, they all managed to struggle up through the immense watery wave creature who had dived over them; and that was a big relief.

"The—the things that happen to a chap out here!" Del exclaimed, tossing his streaming wet hair up off his eyes and glancing about him at a very bedraggled Bushbo and Desert Pea.

But even now it was hard for him to know exactly what was going on or what to think about anything, for he was being rushed along so quickly that everything seemed upside-down and inside-out, and he had certainly not been buffeted about half so much since Willie-willie; and altogether he began to wonder if he would ever be able to see or hear or think straight again.

Then, with a cry of delight, the little red desert pea suddenly grasped the situation and, wriggling the whole of himself out on top of the water, flung his legs over across its back until he was astride it, clinging tightly to it with hands and knees just as if he were riding a rocket. And, seeing this, Del and Bushbo quickly copied him, so that soon they were all as comfortable as could be expected, dashing, one behind the other, over miles and miles of sandy flatness and, now and then, a group of ragged though graceful palms.

"Ah!" said the same frothy voice they had heard once before. "That's sensible, upon my word. I was wondering how long it would take you to gather up a few wits."

"That's sensible, upon my word."

CAUGHT!

"Well, it's a mighty wonder it didn't take us a couple of weeks or something, the way we've been knocked about," Del replied sharply.

Whereupon the air they were rushing through got streaked all over with a sort of hissing laughter, and the goggle-eyed dragon-face looked round at its three small passengers with a long row of wispy, narrow teeth in its smiling mouth and a flash of blue in its eyes. And shooting up from its forehead were two tiny fountains that sprayed out into hundreds of shining droplets, while from the back of its neck a watery mane went flowing out like a veil.

Del edged up closer to Desert Pea, peering around him to get a closer view of this amazing fellow. "And who on earth are you?" he asked.

"Finke!" answered the dragon-face.

"Oh fonk!" Del retorted. "That's no way to answer a chap."

And once again the air was filled with streaming laughter, while the odd creature's teeth looked longer than ever.

"Stupid!" Bushbo leaned forward and whispered merrily in Del's ear. "He wasn't being funny. Finke is his name, don't you know! He's a very large and famous river. Why, he zigzags about like mad right down through Macdonnell Ranges—"

"Say, how he must tickle!" Del burst in excitedly.

"And then," Bushbo continued, looking very sedate, "he stops dead. But it's his bone-dry track we've been following ever since—ever since we left old Ranges, that is."

"Well, I never!" Del exclaimed, peeping round Desert Pea's shoulder again. "You really are real, then, sir?"

"Torrents and thunderbolts, boy, what did you think I was—a myth?"

"Well, y-yes, more or less," Del answered, nervously. " 'Cause you see, Uncle Edward says that dragons—great big ones like you, that is—just don't exist any more these days; only in fairy tales."

"He does, eh? Well, as a matter of fact, boy, there is a bit of the myth about me, I s'pose."

"Not about the way you can knock people about and nearly drown them," Del remarked, looking injured.

And Finke River laughed again, and swished at a madder rate than ever across the yellow sands.

"Say, by the way," Del added, realizing that the mighty river was spending far more time looking back than forward, "do you know where you're going and where you're taking us, or—or don't you care?"

"I know, all right, boy. I know," answered the river, closing his eyes, nodding his head and looking clownishly solemn. "After the last thousands of years, I think you can trust me to know my own track inside-out."

"Great Scott! Have you really been going strong all that time, though?"

"Well, not *all* the time. That's where the myth part comes in." And, with an extra spurt of his forehead fountains and a toss of his long, watery mane, he turned and bounded so abruptly over a small sandhill that Desert Pea went tumbling back against Del, and Del against Bushbo, so that if Bushbo had not kept holding on with every bit of his strength, they might all have gone helter-skeltering through again into Finke's swirling inside.

"Hey!" Del protested indignantly. "What's the idea, funny-face?"

"Hey yourself!" Bushbo murmured. "You might speak to him with more respect, my boy, considering he's the oldest river in all the world."

Del opened his mouth wide, then suddenly closed it again. "Well, I wish he'd be his age," he answered, cocking his head up high, "instead of going on like a—a something or other in the circus."

"Ah, but that's the way of rivers, Del," said the little red desert pea, glancing round almost coyly, "'specially when they can only come to life now and then, like this fellow. You'd want

CAUGHT!

to make the most of it too, if you kept having to be dead for months and months, and coming to life again for a little while only whenever the rain sprites had won a great battle against Desert's sand tribes."

"Gracious!" Del cried out. "And that's what happens to poor old Finke?"

"Yes, to be sure!" Bushbo replied. "And of course, when some people watch and watch and wait and wait and still can't manage to catch him alive for some reason or other, no wonder they begin to think he's dead and gone for keeps."

"And that's the myth part, then?"

"Yes, that's it."

Del frowned. He had a vague idea somewhere in the back of his mind that the flooded old river—the bounding, watery dragon—was going a lot slower now than before, and with not quite so much strength and sureness; but he did not stop to think about this, for there were too many other things puzzling him. So, "Well, but what happens to him all the time he's dead?" he asked.

"Sh!" whispered Desert Pea, putting the tip of a little jet-black finger up against his pursed-together lips. "Another secret, Del, that we've promised not to tell to any mortal—not yet, that is."

"Oh bother your jolly secrets!" Del cried out at the top of his voice. "I – I don't want to know, anyway. See?"

And he had quite a lot more to say while he was about it, only suddenly it was all bumped right out of his mind, for he noticed that he, Bushbo and Desert Pea were sitting, one behind the other and with their legs spread out as far as they would go—no longer on Finke's broad, watery back, but on bone-dry sand. And Del, blinking and staring, saw a few of the tiny yellow grains rushing about on spidery legs, with the wickedest gleam imaginable in their eyes.

For a moment he glowered over them, then he exploded. "You dirty little demons, what've you done with our Finke?" he demanded.

MAGIC AUSTRALIA

But the grubby-faced imps only scuttled away for all they were worth, without answering.

"Great Scott!" Del went on. "What on earth could little things like that have done with him, anyhow? Where on earth's he gone to? That's what I want to know."

"Another secret, I'm afraid," Desert Pea answered softly, then ducked, giggling, as Del shot him a furious glance out of his bright blue eyes.

"But look here, I just don't get it," Del continued, too puzzled about everything to be really annoyed about anything.

Scuttled away without answering.

"A great rushing river like that disappearing all of a sudden and no one'll tell me where to—"

"Ah, but not *quite* all of a sudden, Del," said Desert Pea, shaking his finger at him. "If you hadn't been so busy chatterboxing, you might have seen a good while back that poor old Finke was going slower and slower, what with the millions of sand tribes pulling him under with all their might—"

"Look here, it's a rotten shame, that's what it is. Those dirty little fiends, I—I'd like to string them all out in a line and trip them up or something."

Then, glaring down more closely, Del saw that amongst the sand there were pieces of bluish-whiteness, which crowded closer and closer together, a little farther on, until at last they formed themselves into an enormous lake, big as a sea and blue as the sky, and shimmering in the sunlight as if with millions of

CAUGHT!

silvery crystals. But, having learnt his lesson about lakes in the centre of Australia, he was very careful what he said or thought about this one.

"I say, look! Is that one of those jolly things that aren't?" he asked.

"No," Desert Pea whispered mysteriously. "It's a ghost."

Del ruffled his fair curls and scratched his head. "Ghost of what?" he, also, whispered.

"Of a lake, of course," Bushbo replied. "A lake that used to be. There's quite a number more of them round here, too—just as old Finke has a great brother river who's mostly dead these days, the same as himself, and comes to life with a rush only now-and-thenish."

"Glory! And what's his name?"

"Cooper," said Desert Pea.

Del was silent for a minute or two, thinking, for there were so many queer things everywhere, and such a lot of surprises and adventures, that he felt they were all running ahead of him and that he would have to think hard to keep pace with them. "But now, this lake ghost," he said at last, very boldly, "it's a mighty quiet ghost, isn't it?"

"If you were a ghost you'd be quiet too," said Desert Pea, twinkling.

"Eyre!" Bushbo murmured to himself thoughtfully. "Greatest of all the lake ghosts in this hot and barren plain!"

But Del did not hear him, for he was creeping about on tiptoe along the edge of the huge, shining blueness, growing braver and more pleased with himself every moment.

"Hey!" he shouted back after a while, to Bushbo and Desert Pea who were slowly straggling along behind him. "This is a bonzer ghost—solid enough to have games on, or a picnic or something."

And mentioning a picnic made him think of nice things to eat; and, staring down at the ghost of Lake Eyre, he thought that bits of him would surely be very nice to eat. So, to show

how brave he was feeling, he took the immense liberty of stooping down, scraping off a little piece of the shining stuff and putting it in his mouth. But although it was pretty enough to look at, the ghost of Lake Eyre was so horrid and bitter to taste that the next moment Del was feeling anything except brave and clever and, making an awful face, spat as much of it out as he possibly could.

"Hey, you!" he called back to Bushbo and Desert Pea. "Why couldn't you've told me what he was, this jolly old ghost? He —he's all salt, the old thing! Great Scott, he's awful!"

But Bushbo and Desert Pea were too busy laughing to give

He very nearly jumped inside-out.

him an answer. And in any case, Del was in no mood to stand waiting for one, for suddenly he got a terrible fright.

Looking down at the enormous lake ghost and scowling, he very nearly jumped inside-out with shock, for there, staring up at him and also scowling, was a most extraordinary face—a face

CAUGHT!

that was all glittering and blue and angry, with a pointed beak of a nose, and a bald sparkling head and gleaming white teeth, and flashing blue eyes something like Finke's, only much sharper and crueller-looking. And the whole tremendous head was lying back on a couple of folded hands, which must have been very long indeed, for Del caught a glimpse of the pointed fingers, with their white sparkling nails, peeping out from either side.

Too surprised to make even the smallest remark, and so frightened that his heart was bobbing up and down all over the place like a balloon, Del instantly spun round on his heels, and tried to run as he had never run before, over the huge blue ghost that seemed to have no end. But he soon found that he could not run fast at all, for he kept tripping and slithering as if he were on ice; and also, every now and then, crashing through the surface he had thought to be so solid into thick, horrible mud. And as it seemed that this mud kept sucking at him, trying to drag him down into its stifling heart, he spent far more time and energy pulling himself out of it than making any headway. In spite of this, however, he continued stumbling on as fast as possible. Even the sound of Bushbo's and Desert Pea's laughter, following him up and ringing in his ears, made no difference to him. He ran on just the same. If they had seen what he had, he told himself stoutly, they wouldn't be feeling so clever or making so much noise.

But the very next moment poor Del had forgotten all about the angry ghost of Lake Eyre, and this was how it happened:

"Here, I'll give you a help on, young man!" called a strange, muffled voice he had not heard before—a voice that sounded as if it must be buried underneath a dozen powdery blankets of dust.

Terrified beyond all measure, Del gave one glance back over his shoulder, then shouted out a frantic, piercing. "Bushbo! Bushbo!" For there, bowling after him, towering high and spreading wide, was a great, sooty-coloured living wheel, hard and grimy all over, with a mop of tangled hair on his head, and a broad face wrinkled up with laughter. And he was carrying a huge bag, which went flying out behind him at the end of a long string.

"Oh. heavens!" Del muttered between his teeth. "How all these chaps find such a lot to laugh at I—I don't know. And why they've all got to be so big I—I don't know either."

A great sooty-coloured living wheel.

And he kept on running faster and faster, and getting more and more out of breath, and every now and then calling out shrilly to Bushbo. But no help or answer ever came, and it was quite useless for a pair of nine-year-old little boy legs to race that giant sooty wheel who was now, in any case, right on top of him.

CAUGHT!

"Ow, help!" Del shouted, as he was suddenly snatched up and thrown down head-first into the great dark bag.

But of course, no one took any notice, and for a few minutes he rolled and tumbled about in the darkness, grunting, snorting and puffing, not able to think of any intelligent sound at all, and feeling the whole time more and more stifled, hot, dirty and generally uncomfortable. Then he bumped against something that felt like somebody's leg, and immediately there was a burst of merry laughter that he well knew. He had actually bumped into the little red desert pea.

"Say," Del exclaimed, wild with relief, "this is fun! Is Bushbo here too?"

"Yes," came Bushbo's own voice through the choking dust and darkness. "I'm here, sure enough. Don't quite know how any one could help being here. When fierce old Dust-storm comes along, you might just as well give up and let him do what he likes with you; for if you don't, he'll do what he likes with you just the same."

"Dust-storm! So that's who he is!" said Del. "What a strong, fuzzy-looking chap! And how he can just about stifle a fellow! Does he often come dashing about here like this?"

"My word, he does—very often," Desert Pea piped in. Then he caught his breath and coughed and coughed, until Del thought that he might easily burst open Dust-storm's giant bag and let all three of them out. He didn't, though.

"And—and is he dangerous, this chap?" Del asked, trying to sound unconcerned.

"Oh," said Bushbo, "that all depends. If he were in the mood he might keep you buried inside this wretched bag of his until you were suffocated; and if you had a farm all planted out with things, he'd most likely carry it away just the same as Willie-willie would. Oh, all sorts of exciting things he might do." he ended up cheerily.

"Gracious goodness alive!" said Del, and meant it as he had

never meant it before; and, in the darkness where neither Bushbo nor Desert Pea could see him, he gave a little gulp and bit his underlip. But then, immediately, he cocked up his head and thrust both his hands deep down into his pockets, fingering the many treasures there; and, leaning back against the gritty, whirling bag, he softly whistled a few snatches of Uncle Edward's favourite tune.

CHAPTER X

DARTING FLAME

"LOOK!" Desert Pea called out all of a sudden; for, unknown to Del and Bushbo, he had been exploring for some time past, and had now found what he was looking for. "I've got a peephole."

Instantly there was a mad scramble, and his two friends were swarming all over him, and the next moment his peephole was covered in by Bushbo's nut-brown head.

"Ferns and mosses!" Bushbo exclaimed. "Here, Del, look at this!" And, grabbing Del by the shoulders, he shoved him up against the tiny hole. "See?" he asked.

"Oh, I say!" Del answered, and tried—which was very difficult indeed—to fix his eyes upon this, one of the prettiest things he had ever seen.

First of all he thought it was a huge butterfly, or humming-bird, for it was not still for a single second, but kept darting to and fro, up and down, and round in spasmodic circles. When after a minute or two, though, it happened to shoot right up next to the peephole for the tiniest possible instant, he saw that it was no such thing, but a frail, bright girl spirit quivering all over like vibrant flame. Her skin was like a flower petal with the sunset glowing through it, her short wispy frock seemed to light up with her every movement in the most surprising flashes of green and blue, and her long sparkling hair was the colour of bronze and gold.

Del could not say a single word. He could only hold his breath and feel sure that he must be dreaming—and even surer

MAGIC AUSTRALIA

still when, a moment afterwards, the strange, darting spirit was nowhere to be seen.

"Oh Bushbo, Bushbo!" he cried, trembling with excitement. "What was it? Was—was there really someone out there just now, or—"

"Of course there was," Bushbo replied with a laugh. "Very much there. And one of Australia's loveliest creatures, too."

"Glory, yes!" Del agreed with deep feeling.

"She's Opal, you know," Bushbo added.

"Opal!" Del repeated softly. "Say, the one who cast the spell over my cockle-shell thousands of years ago?"

"The very same, old chap."

"Oh, heavens!" And Del flattened his face up against the peephole once more, peering eagerly through the clouds of sand and dust that kept for ever swishing past him and stinging his eyes. For he must, he felt—he simply must see her again, even if only once and for the merest second. But, search as he might in every possible direction, he could see nothing except dust and sand.

A frail, bright girl spirit.

"Oh, Bushbo," he murmured, "how can we ever find her again?" And he sounded so tired and downhearted that Bushbo and Desert Pea both felt quite sorry for him, and Desert Pea fumbled his way up and placed a gentle little hand upon his arm.

DARTING FLAME

"Never mind, Del!" he said. "Opal's just like that, you know. She follows no well-worn track as old Finke does. In fact, she very seldom follows any sort of a track at all. She just pops up here and there in the most surprising places, and scarcely ever where she's expected. Oh, I've known men go almost mad trying to find her."

Del sighed. It was a sigh that sounded strangely like a sob.

"Look here, come on, now!" Bushbo brought in warmly. "Don't take it to heart so. Sure enough she's as glorious as a magic-maker's dream; but she's a creature of fancy, Del—"

"I—I think I like fancy, though," Del protested feebly. "Sometimes, anyway—"

"Yes," said the little red desert pea, "but Opal's fancy is only ever her own—not any one else's."

And just then, about a couple of inches away, out there amongst the flying greyness, Del suddenly glimpsed a flash of fiery green, and, gripping the fuzzy inside of Dust-storm's bag, he stared and stared until his head ached and his whole self felt tired, then, with a sad little whimper, he turned away and flung himself face downwards, and thought he would never care any more about anything.

"Oh, come on. Del! This is awful," said Desert Pea after some time.

But Del took not the slightest notice.

"My, how old Dusty can travel, eh? Just look at the way we're flying along!" Bushbo cried out enthusiastically.

But Del said nothing at all—only sniffed a little in the darkness.

And so, every little while, both Desert Pea and Bushbo did all they could to make Del forget Opal and feel better. But no, he could not forget her, and certainly nothing made him feel better.

Then finally, gazing through the peephole, Bushbo saw something that he was sure would do the trick even if nothing else could, and, "Well I never!" he exclaimed. "If it isn't Flinders

MAGIC AUSTRALIA

Range himself, beaming away there for all he's worth—and that's a mighty lot. Look, Del! Macdonnell Ranges's own brother, trying to hold the fort down here in the south against wicked old Desert—and making a pretty good job of it, too."

But Del was no more interested in Flinders Range than he was in anything else.

"Oh, come on, Del! Come and have a look at him while you can. He's even a brighter coloured giant than his brother up north. And as for being rich—you don't know what riches mean until you've seen Flinders."

But still Del took no notice.

"You never know what might happen if you got up and yelled out to him that you were here," Bushbo went on. "Why, he might even throw something to wretched old Dust-storm to hand over to you—something to put with your collection. A bit of silver-lead or copper or asbestos, maybe, or perhaps another piece of gold—anything from the cone of a pine-tree to a speck of magic radium. Goodness knows what he might give you—maybe something that no one's ever dreamt of yet. His treasure-house is just about the richest you could imagine, and chock-a-block with mysteries. He hasn't told any one half of what he's got there yet."

So when, after all this, Del's only reply was another little sniff, no wonder was it that Bushbo and Desert Pea gave up trying to do anything with him, and let themselves be carried on for ever and ever so long in silence.

"I say, Bushlands," the little red desert pea brought in at last. "I'm getting worried. If Dusty goes on like this much longer—well, I'll be quite lost, I'm afraid."

"Goodness knows what the fellow's got in mind," Bushbo declared irritably, for being worried as he was about Del made him very short-tempered indeed. "I've been more or less keeping an eye on things all this time, but the way he's twirled round everywhere has made it mighty difficult. He's going towards the west now, though."

DARTING FLAME

"The west!" Desert Pea exclaimed excitedly. "Oh, Bushlands, are you sure—quite sure?"

"Well, almost," Bushbo replied solemnly.

"What *is* all that muttering going on down there?" suddenly demanded Dust-storm's own thick, woolly voice, as he dragged open the top of his bag and squinted down into it with one screwed-up eye.

"Oh, Dusty, Dusty!" cried the little red desert pea, jumping up and down, and shining blacker and redder than ever. "Are we really going to Nullarbor?"

At which Dust-storm merely laughed and winked and, pulling shut his bag again, spun over and over so many times that soon his three small passengers were thoroughly giddy and befuzzled. But as he spun and rolled and tumbled, and they with him, they kept hearing snatches of his merry, muffled song—a song which seemed to have an endless number of verses, every one of which ended with a queer, throbbing whisper, "So on we go to Nullarbor!"

"Say, Bushbo, what's Nullarbor?" Del murmured, at last showing a pinpoint of interest in something. "I—I remember Uncle Edward talking about it once, but—"

"Well, just you wait and see!" Bushbo quickly answered, now properly happy for the first time in the last hour or so.

"And see, too, that after this you never forget again what mighty Nullarbor is—if you can," he added mysteriously.

CHAPTER XI

THE PALACE OF NULLARBOR

IT seemed a very long time indeed before anything else happened after this—anything else except rolling and tumbling. So that when Dusty did at last stop for a moment and tip his passengers out, they were all so happy to have escaped from the heat and stuffiness of his bag that they were ready to feel enthusiastic about anything—even another great wasteland of sand and rockiness, and dwarfed scrubby plants and absolute dryness.

"Thank you, O Dust-storm!" Bushbo cried out. "You've brought us just where I was wanting to come."

"Me too!" exclaimed Desert Pea. "It's wonderful here when the rain sprites have just had a diving spell—which they have now, although it doesn't quite look like it."

"Yes, isn't it?" piped a tiny voice, high and sweet.

And, looking round quickly, the three friends saw a dear little girl standing on tiptoe right beside them. All over she was the colour of snow-flakes, and her head was covered with short white curls, and she wore a pure-white dress made from dozens of stiff, papery-looking peaks, that stood straight out all round her as if she were a fairy dancer.

"Daisy dear!" said the little red desert pea, clasping his hands together, and his eyes lighting up with joy.

"Catch me!" cried the little maiden playfully. And turning, she darted off like a shooting star, with Desert Pea, her favourite playmate, after her. Far out over the sand and stones they raced, shouting and laughing, and making the whole place look alive with their flashing colours.

THE PALACE OF NULLARBOR

"When it's wet, many thousands of other flowers run and dance about over these sad plains," Bushbo, watching them, said wistfully. But Del was more interested in Dust-storm at the moment than in the little red desert pea or the little maiden, for that strange, quiet, tumbling mass of dirty greyness was rollicking off so quickly into the distance that Del could scarcely see the human shape it had seemed to have before, with the big rugged head meeting the big rugged feet as the whole rugged body threw itself round into the form of a wheel. Now it looked merely like a rolling cloud of dust, and for a moment he

Far out over the sand and stones they raced.

wondered if it could ever really have been anything else, but deep inside himself he knew quite well that it had been.

Then suddenly he realized that there was a queer whirring noise going on somewhere near by and, after listening intently for a moment, "Whatever is it, Bushbo?" he whispered. "Sounds spooky enough for anything."

The golden-brown boy laughed. "It's Nullarbor calling us," he said. "Look! See? Calling us through here."

And, looking down, Del noticed for the first time that he was standing nearly on the edge of a dark hole all jagged with rocks and just big enough for a boy to be able to fall right into it; and there was a musty smell coming up out of it in what he could almost imagine to be pale clouds of vapour. He took a little hitch of a breath, and crept back a step or two. And still the queer rumbling sounds went on, babbling and echoing in a language he had never heard before.

"But—but what do you mean it's Nullarbor calling us?" he stammered. "I thought this was Nullarbor, up here, where Dusty landed us. And—and Desert Pea seemed to think so, too," he added eagerly, anxious to assure Bushbo that the weird voice coming up through the rocky hole had nothing whatever to do with them.

But, "Oh no," Bushbo replied. "This isn't the real Nullarbor —not by any means. People used to think it was, but now they know it isn't, though they haven't explored much yet—scarcely at all, in fact!"

"No, there—there really isn't any need to, is there, Bushbo?" Del remarked quickly.

"Why, Del!" said Bushbo with a grin. "You're so bad! Poor Nullabor; as it is, he can only fret and fume his life away deep down under the ground here, while we are above him, standing over his palace roof."

And Del, looking, did see. "But what on earth are you talking about?" he asked, frowning. "What palace? You're mad, Bushbo!"

"Come and find out for yourself," Bushbo answered promptly. "This way. I'll go first." And he swung himself down into the dark gap, feeling round for footholds. But Del only sidled back another step and felt hot all over.

"Oh come on, you big silly! Not scared, are you?"

Del kicked a little round pebble and watched it spinning along the sand and rockiness until it stopped. Then, casually, he strolled over to the hole and, feeling hotter than ever, he

THE PALACE OF NULLARBOR

gingerly scrambled down one or two ledges, Bushbo having by now almost disappeared.

No sooner had he got this far, however, than there came a rushing bellow of air from down below, which very nearly blew him all to pieces. Up flew his hair, as straight and high as a family of young telegraph poles; and up also flew Del, to the top of the hole again, in quite quarter the time it had taken him to scramble down.

And up also flew Del.

But instead of any one expressing any sympathy or concern for him after his terrible fright, there came pealing up to him only the sound of Bushbo's laughter—laughter jollier than Del had ever heard from him before, and echoing strangely as if through halls of emptiness.

"You great stupid, Del! Gullies and Waterfalls, you're as scared as a little mouse!"

"L-little mouse yourself!" Del retorted heatedly, going as near to the edge of the hole as he dared. "H-how would you like it if- if—"

"Yes, yes, I know what happened," Bushbo's voice burst in merrily. "Happened to me too, of course. Happens to every one. Well, what odds? It's only Nullarbor's way—"

"Strikes me all you p-people have pretty funny ways," Del remarked angrily. "P-pretty senseless, too."

"Senseless? Good heavens, boy! You blow bubbles, don't you?"

Del did not answer—merely shifted a little from one foot to the other.

"Well," Bushbo continued, "Nullarbor just blows. What's the difference? He's got to have his bit of a joke the same as you. You have a pipe. He's only got a hole, poor fellow!"

Again Del made no reply.

"Well," Bushbo's voice added airily after a few seconds, "if you're coming, come. If you're not, don't." And the faint sound of more scrambling followed.

"Oh bother!" Del muttered under his breath. And without another word he strode boldly down into the hole again and from ledge to ledge, whether he could see where he was going or not, and no matter how much old Nullarbor "just blew". Even when something that might, from the sound of it, have been a bogy-man hobgoblin, shuffled and booted right beside him and, looking round, he saw the two gleaming eyes of what was really an owl glaring across at him—even when this happened, he tried not to care, and only scuttled down over the rocks faster than ever. Then:

"Hey, Bushbo! Wait on, can't you? Wh-where on earth are you?" he panted at last, out of breath and still very frightened inside, especially when he heard his own voice sounding about three times louder than it usually did, and echoing on and on for ever into emptiness.

THE PALACE OF NULLARBOR

In fact, it sounded so huge and different that for a moment he almost expected to find that it had come to life and was stalking after him in some new form of grinning giant. So many extraordinary things had happened to him of late that he would scarcely have been surprised at anything.

Instead of this, however, he heard Bushbo's reassuring —though also tremendously loud—voice calling back to him. "Here I am, old chap," it said. "I'm waiting for you, all right. Just keep on going."

And suddenly Del's heart felt a lot warmer and larger than it had for some time past, and down he went scrambling for all he was worth.

"Great Scott, how much farther?" he shouted, after a few minutes. "I must've come down yards and yards already."

"Hm, about ten of them, I s'pose," answered Bushbo's voice, almost beside him.

And Del, with a tiny gasp of relief, flung himself down towards it, not bothering to wonder, in his excitement, where he might land. When, like the snap of a great jaw, something grabbed both his legs at once, sending him sprawling over the rocky floor and shouting for help at the top of his voice—which was now very high indeed.

But Bushbo's laughter easily out-shouted him. "Trees and mountains, Del!" he exclaimed. "I've never known any one as good as you to tease. Don't you know yet what your old Bushbo's hands feel like?"

And Del, now free, and standing up as steadily as he could after his awful fright and in the darkness that seemed to be spinning around him, did not answer for a moment, then muttered between his teeth, "You wait! You just wait!"

"All right," said Bushbo, taking his hand, at which Del gave another little start. "But in the meantime, let's get on a bit. We're almost there."

"Where?"

"You'll see."

Together they took a few more steps, treading carefully on

the uneven ground. Then, turning a corner, they found themselves standing at the entrance of what seemed to be a huge empty room, filled with a pale glimmer of light.

"Whatever is it?" Del breathed. "Where are we?"

"This," Bushbo whispered back, "is where the real Nullarbor lives. This is a tiny bit of his vast palace—just one of its rooms. Goodness knows how many hundreds of them there are altogether."

"Glory!" said Del.

"Come on, let's explore a bit!" Bushbo suggested, stepping boldly forward into the centre of the room, with Del dragging behind him, wide-eyed and hoppity-hearted. "Big, isn't it?" said Bushbo.

"Yes," said Del, "and c-c-cold, too—like ice or s-s-something."

"And still!" Bushbo added in a hushed, lingering tone. "As still as death."

Del shuddered, and then gripped Bushbo's arm with both his hands and clung to him in terror, for suddenly the words they had whispered began to echo through the room. Not in an ordinary way, however, but as if they had been caught up by the huge, endless past, and dropped one by one, separately, slowly, to settle at last into a little tower of solid whiteness—into hundreds and hundreds of little towers of solid whiteness, until the whole room was filled with them.

So that as Del and Bushbo grew more used to this particular kind of pale darkness in Nullarbor's underground palace, they found that they were standing amid a perfect forest of white towers, some tall, others tiny, but all of them graceful and tapering. Many of them went rearing up from the rocky floor, many others came swinging down, peak first, from the rocky ceiling, and quite a number of them did both together, so that they formed whole columns between floor and ceiling.

"Cold and still! Cold and still!" repeated the clear, timeless voice. "But not like death. For me there is no death."

"Listen!" said Bushbo. "The voice of Nullarbor!"

THE PALACE OF NULLARBOR

"What, the chap who blows just for the sake of it?" Del asked in a hoarse whisper.

"Yes. But he's not always in a frivolous mood, of course."

And there were a lot more things that Del wanted to know about, but he did not feel quite brave enough to keep on asking questions; so, for a moment, he merely stood and gazed—all round the dim, cold, ghostly room, from one to another of the countless icicle-like peaks. And then, looking more closely and with his heart bobbing about inside him faster than ever, he saw that there was a smile amongst those peaks—a thin, pointy smile, with several of them jutting down into a chin and one into a nose, while sweeping up over the ceiling were two long, white arms with sleeves fringing down into more of the same odd peaks, and over on the other side of the large room two great white hands plunged down into space, a peak for every finger.

"G-g-g-glory!" he stammered. "Say, Bushbo, I c-c-can't ever get used to these jolly things. They're—they're a bit too much for a chap, I tell you!"

And suddenly every one of the white peaks and columns in the cave room began to shimmer, just as if it had thousands of crystals embedded in it, until the whole place quivered with innumerable twinkles and looked very pretty and magic indeed.

But Del, who could only feel trapped in a great, dark world full of white, pointing fingers and a ghostly smile, was more frightened than ever. "Oh, I say! Whatever's happening now?" he muttered.

"Old Nullarbor's laughing, of course," said Bushbo.

Del slowly scratched the back of his head. "Does *everybody* laugh out here?" he demanded, a trifle irritably.

"Yes," Bushbo replied. "Even the saddest and loneliest parts can laugh. Why, didn't you know, Del? Australia's a land of laughter. And a marvellous gift it is too, isn't it, Nullarbor?"

And Del, watching, saw the smile among the white peaks widen, and the shimmering grow faster and brighter. And he crept closer to Bushbo, just the tiniest bit.

MAGIC AUSTRALIA

"When you're as old for a human as Australia is for a country —if you ever are, that is—" Bushbo continued, also smiling, "you'll have learnt the real art and value of laughter, won't he, Nullarbor?"

And now the two drooping eyes on either side of the long

There was a smile amongst those peaks.

white nose slowly closed themselves, in such a way that one could almost see the head belonging to them nodding wisely, while "Indeed!" answered the timeless voice, dropping another crystal word upon the top of one of the little white towers. And then again, "Indeed!" it echoed.

But to Del a talking, laughing cave, cold and white as a ghost, and far—ever so far—down in the dungeon-like centre of the

THE PALACE OF NULLARBOR

earth, was unspeakably terrifying. And although he tried not to show this, Nullarbor seemed to know all about it, for suddenly, opening his eyes again, he asked, "Why do you fear me, laddie? Have you never visited my brother caves in the east—comfortably nestling down among the mountains you call Blue, and watched over by Eastern Bushlands here?"

"Y-yes, sir, I have," Del answered in an odd, squeaky voice. "Uncle Edward t-t-took me once."

"Oh he did, did he, laddie? And tell me, what did you think of them? Did they frighten you?"

"No, they d-d-didn't," Del answered promptly. "They were great. But then, they were all l-lighted up, and had steps going down into them, and they m-made you feel quite happy about everything—not as if they might g-gobble you up any minute, or g-g-grab you, or something. And they were nice and cool, but not f-f-freezing, sir."

"Well, I'm not altogether as good-looking as my brothers in the east. I'll readily admit that, laddie. But mind you, I'm not bad. No, I quite agree with you, I'm not bad at all."

And then Nullarbor seemed to fade away; search and stare as he might, and, as he got braver, call and shout as he might, Dell could no longer see any face or arms or fingers anywhere. "Hey, Nullarbor!" he cried out. "What've you gone and done with yourself? Nullarbor! Here, come back! I want to talk to you."

But the only things he could see were countless long, white towers uprising and downrooping all over the palace cave room, and a few stout, grooved columns.

Exasperated, he scratched viciously at the back of his head. "Where on earth's he gone?" he demanded. "And—and how did he get away? And look here, why does everybody have to do things like this? It puts a chap right out, I tell you. A-a chap never knows where he is. I mean," he added, mumbling under his breath and strutting about very boldly, glaring separately at one peak after another, "it does make a fellow feel awfully silly to find he's been talking away for dear life to—to nothing at all."

But Bushbo, beaming merrily, hurried across to him and, grabbing him by the arm, motioned him to silence.

"Why, what's the matter now?" Del demanded indignantly.

"Listen, little silly!" Bushbo replied. Then, after a few seconds, "Can't you hear?"

"Heavens, yes!" Del whispered, a tiny shiver pirouetting down his spine. "Wh-what is it?"

"Come and we'll see."

"Oh, but—well, do you think we really need?" Del burst out quickly. "It—it's sure to be nothing much," he added.

Bushbo, however, seemed to think differently, for he rapidly strode off, threading his way among the pointed towers, in the direction the sound seemed to be coming from, dragging Del after him. And there, in one piece of the wall, was a large, rugged opening, all moist and rocky, which led through into more darkness—the blackest darkness so far. And now the sound came clearer than ever, babbling, gurgling, frothing, hissing, like dozens of watery voices all arguing on top of one another.

"There! You see?" said Del, trying to ignore it all. "Just what I told you! All quite dark. Nothing to be seen. And—and by the way, it's high time we were getting back up top again. Must be awfully late."

"Oh, no you don't!" Bushbo replied, grinning to himself. "Come on, little white one. We're going to explore."

And it was useless for Del to protest any further. He was simply dragged along. On and on over slimy, uneven ground they tripped, slipped and stumbled, never seeing an inch ahead of them and never speaking a word to each other, but always with the watery voices coming nearer and nearer to them, until suddenly these seemed to fill every bit of space that anything could be heard in, and there, rushing past them and roaring along its rocky banks was a huge black river—black because of the darkness everywhere.

"Oh, glory! Oh, Bushbo!" cried poor Del. And he felt so

THE PALACE OF NULLARBOR

nervous that his foot slipped, and down he went right into it as far as one knee. Before he could get down any farther, however, Bushbo gripped him tightly and pulled him up again.

"The pickles I save you from, old chap!" he exclaimed, laughing. "You really ought to be very grateful to me, you know."

"If-if it wasn't for you," Del shouted back, "there—there wouldn't be any pickles. And you wouldn't be l-laughing so much, either, if *you'd* slipped in. It—it's just like ice, the beastly stuff! I'm frozen, I tell you."

"Well, well, well!" they both heard the loud voice of the river suddenly declare.

Whereupon Del sprang back behind Bushbo and, shivering slightly, peered round to see if anything was happening. And sure enough, rearing itself up from the river, higher and higher into the blackness, was an even darker blackness, with a gleam of white teeth in its mouth and of white sparkles in its eyes, and with altogether a decided likeness to the cave face as it smiled at its two visitors.

"So you think I'm beastly stuff, do you, my fine young human?"

"Oh n-n-no, sir!" Del quickly assured him with chattering teeth. "I was r-really only joking."

"And a good thing for you, too!" answered the smiling blackness. "Although I don't know. Even now I've a jolly good mind to grab you with my icy hands and rush you along with my current fifty miles or so right to the edge of the map, then tip you into the sea. How would you like that, eh?"

"Oh, Bushbo, Bushbo!" Del pleaded, throwing his arms completely around the older boy's waist and burying his head in his back, so that his words came out all choked and woolly. "Don't let him! Please, please don't let him! I—I'm scared."

"Why, you poor old chap!" Bushbo answered good-naturedly. "Don't you recognize our friend of the cave room—just the same good old Nullarbor in another part of his palace?"

"Yes," agreed the blackness, "the very same—flowing and languishing and building and hoarding, way down here in my underground palace of caves and rivers, almost since the beginning of time."

"Don't you recognize our friend of the cave room?"

"Flowing all this way underground?" Del said, now quite forgetting his terror, but still clinging to Bushbo through habit. "You too, sir? Just like water?"

"Yes," said the blackness, "just like those calm, beautiful water spirits who sit the centuries away at the bottoms of huge underground wells.

And, with a deep, gurgling sigh, the rearing dark head sank down once more into the rushing river and disappeared, beginning over again all the old arguing and protesting in a language no mortal could understand.

"It-it does seem jolly queer, doesn't it?" Del exclaimed after a short silence. "All this water under the ground here, and up there everything bone-dry—"

THE PALACE OF NULLARBOR

"Except now-and-thenish, after a shower of rain sprites." Bushbo brought in.

"I would really enjoy it more where it's a lot wetter and things can live all year long" said Del.

"You know, that's not a bad idea," Bushbo told him, suddenly enthusiastic again. "There's all the glorious tropical north we haven't been to yet, where the earth spirit and the rain sprites are so generous that the plains are thick green carpets and the forests great entanglements of growth and colour. My word, Del, by all the ferns and mosses in my own fair gullies, we're going there, you and I.."

Del's heart bounded with delight and eagerness. He and Bushbo off together on the same quest! And now to get out of this cold, dark, slippery, echoing palace of caves and rivers! "But how?" Del asked himself with great misgiving. "Gracious to goodness, how?"

CHAPTER XII

THE CORAL KINGDOM

ALONG one winding passage after another and the banks of several icy rivers, and through an endless number of cave rooms, Del and Bushbo stumbled, always in darkness with only the merest glimmer of light now and then. And at last, so tired that he felt he could not walk another inch, Del sat down on a cold, slippery rock, with tears stinging in his eyes.

"Oh, glory!" he said, his voice trembling with annoyance as well as with tiredness. "I'm that sick of this, I could howl. What'll we do, Bushbo? Say, lost in a place like this! Why can't old Nullarbor turn up again somewhere and show us how to get out? What's the matter with him? Does he think we want to keep wandering round here for ever?"

"He might," answered Bushbo. And, sitting down also, he wished and wished that Del would think of going to sleep, for he too was tired of being lost in the darkness, and it was only when Del's mortal part was asleep that Bushbo could get some magic to work on his mind part. And that was all that was needed; for once the thinking and feeling Del was properly carried away anywhere, the mortal Del followed as a matter of course.

So, it was just like an answer to what Bushbo was wishing most when Del, mumbling a little, curled himself up where he was and announced that before he walked another step he would jolly well have a sleep.

And sleep he did—for so long, in fact, that Bushbo thought he would never wake up. But when at last he did open his eyes

THE CORAL KINGDOM

and blink them a few times, he was feeling fit for anything and in a very good humour indeed.

Then, with a jerk, he realized how funny everything was, and how he had never seen anything quite like this before, and how he was no longer in Nullarbor's dark palace of caves and rivers, but in a queer place of swaying movements and bluey-green light.

"Hey, Bushbo!" he called out, seeing his friend standing near by and beaming down at him. "What's the idea? Can't a chap possibly go to sleep and wake up in the same spot out here? Must he—" But suddenly he stopped, and opened his eyes rounder than ever, for he noticed that, as he spoke, a flock of little bubbles went floating up out of his mouth at a mad, sparkling pace—up, up, up, ever so high. And when Bushbo laughed at him a flock of little bubbles came dashing out of his mouth, too.

"Oh, you'll soon get used to *them*, Del," he said.

"Great Scott! We must be under the sea, or something," Del shouted, springing to his feet.

"We are," said Bushbo.

"We—we can't be, though!" Del retorted. "You know perfectly well we couldn't breathe and talk like this at the bottom of the sea. I couldn't, anyway."

"Hm. Well, maybe you'll never be able to again," said Bushbo. "But in the meantime—"

And by now the bubbles from both their mouths were capering up after each other quite riotously.

Del watched them, for the moment speechless. Then warily he began to peer about him, and discovered to his unbounded surprise that he was in the middle of the most wonderful garden he had ever seen, full of bright colours and strange, beautiful things that looked as if they might have been ordinary plants had not some Wizard mischiefed them. Some were like ferns, only brilliant red or purple—which seemed wrong, somehow.

Others were like trees with tangling branches. Only they were all pink or blue or yellow. Some, growing in rock crevices, were like flowers, only that each petal seemed to sway and quiver singly as if it had a separate life of its own. Others were like mushrooms, only that they were giant affairs and had all their raying frills on top instead of underneath. And darting in amongst them with flashing colours and fluttering wings were what might have been hundreds of birds and butterflies, only that they were fish instead, and their wings were really fins.

"Wh-what *I* still want to know," Del declared at last, "is how we can be here. We—we just can't be, see? It must be one of those mirage things—something that isn't."

But Bushbo only laughed at him—and somebody else laughed too.

Del, startled, quickly looked round in every possible direction, but for a long time could not see who it was. Then, all at once, he did see; and it was scarcely to be wondered at that he had not been able to pick her out sooner, for she looked just like a tiny part of the strange, vivid garden all round him—that narrow little figure with her graceful arms branching up over her head in a waking-up kind of stretch, and her legs folded under her as she sat, smiling though dreamy-eyed, on the sandy, rocky ground.

Del stared at her, puzzled and delighted. All over—from the wee short curls on her head to the tips of her fingers and toes—she was greeny-blue in colour, much the same as the water; and most of her was so curiously and finely patterned that she looked almost like some rare old lace. And nestling in her hair was one of the all-separately-alive flowers—a pale yellow one—whilst a goggle-eyed little fish, turquoise-blue, sat calmly on her shoulder, gazing out at the two boys inquisitively and blinking every now and then.

Del, also, stood blinking for a while. Then, "You—you wouldn't be a mermaid, I s'pose, miss?" he murmured—and

THE CORAL KINGDOM

blushed to the roots of his hair, for it did make a chap feel awfully silly to talk about mermaids. Yet, under the circumstances, what else could a chap do?

But, "Oh, no! Oh dear, no!" the little lass answered. "Surely you must recognize me. I'm very famous. I'm Coral—spirit of the great northern Barrier."

"Barrier?" Del repeated, rather dazed.

"Yes. Haven't you heard of Australia's Barrier Reef?"

"Course I have. Uncle Edward and I have talked about it lots of times."

"Well," she said proudly, "now you can see me as well as talk about me." And she smoothed back a little green curl.

"But—but you're only small," Del objected, frowning, "and the Barrier Reef's as big as big."

"Yes, there are more than a thousand miles of it," she agreed thoughtfully. "And all of it is me, because all of it I've built—every inch of it. And what you've made, with all your heart and soul, is yourself—even more than yourself is."

"Heavens!" said Del. "That sounds like a riddle if anything does."

And she and Bushbo laughed merrily, at which dozens of rainbow-coloured bubbles went dancing after one another on tiptoe—up, up, into bluey-green nothingness.

"More than a thousand miles of Barrier Reef, and you built it all?" Del repeated, his voice high-pitched. "But however long did it take you?"

"Oh, ages and ages," she answered slowly. "Aeons and aeons. Thousands upon thousands of years. But come, let me show you some of my treasures!" she added brightly. And up to her feet she sprang, making Del blink faster than ever, for suddenly she was no longer a demure little green-blue, lace-gowned maiden, but a whirling dancer all golden-brown in colour, the same as Bushbo, and wearing a short, full dress gathered in at her waist, that stood straight out all round her as she spun, so that she looked exactly like one of the giant mushrooms come to life. And, twirling around her in darting spasms wherever she went, was a handsome young fish of cream and brown stripes, with waving, streaming, billowing veils of gossamer flying out from him in all directions.

But even as he watched and wondered, Del saw, standing where the golden brown mushroom dancer had been, a shy little lady very much like the greeny-blue one, only a sweet rose-pink instead, and even slenderer, with a frail upstanding fringe around her neck, and another spraying out around each wrist and ankle, while perched on her shoulder was a lovely rose-pink fish.

"Come!" she called, beckoning to the two boys. "Aren't you coming with me?"

"Oh, but look here!" Del cried out. "Are you still you, after all that?"

"Of course I'm still me," she assured him.

The golden-brown mushroom dancer.

laughing. "I'm scarcely ever in the same mood for two minutes together. You'll soon get used to that."

"And you always choose your pets to match?" Del asked.

"What, my little fish? Oh dear, no! They choose me to match —the darlings!—for they know that if we're the same colour the big bad fish that eat them won't be able to find them nearly so easily, and will most likely pass them by as mere bits of me."

"Wise little fish!" said Bushbo. And they all walked on together through the strange garden of tall swaying seaweeds, and of beautiful rockeries in which every rock was quite round and looked as if someone had carved it all over into fine, cobwebby patterns. And there were avenues of dwarf trees of every colour in the rainbow, while Coral herself seemed to change into everything by turn—even into one of the little round rocks—and into every imaginable colour.

So it was altogether a most entertaining journey for Del and Bushbo, especially with hundreds and thousands of fish streaking, swimming, hopping and gliding everywhere in all the different shapes, sizes, colours and patterns that any one could ever dream of. There were some that looked like balloons, others like fluttering bundles of frills and flounces, some like lollies and others like giant dragonflies. Some looked coy and others savage, some scowled and others smiled; but all of them together, flashing about in the most unexpected ways and places, were just like a magician's jewels—and Bushbo said so, much to Coral's joy and pride, for she loved her little fish pets.

At that very moment, however, it seemed as if something terrible was about to happen, for instead of shooting and fluttering contentedly to and fro and nowhere in particular, they suddenly all came streaming past in one swift mass with the most terrified expressions in their eyes; and in almost a couple of seconds not one of them was to be seen anywhere, and in their place there was only a looming silence and stillness.

"Whatever's the idea?" Del demanded.

But neither Bushbo nor Coral had time to answer him before a great dark shadow came gliding round a rocky corner with an open, cruel-looking mouth and sly, dangerous eyes.

Del was so terror-stricken that he could neither speak nor move, but the whole of him felt stretched to the limit, and he spread all his fingers out stiffly and held his breath. For there, slipping past only a few inches away from him, was a huge grey shark. He knew it was a shark, for he had often looked at pictures of them in some of Uncle Edward's wonderful books. And oh, the dreadful, dreadful stories that Uncle Edward had told him about them! So that the very name of one would have been enough to frighten any little boy, let alone the sight of it only a few inches away from his nose.

But Bushbo leaned one arm around his shoulder and smiled broadly. "Don't worry, old chap!" he cried out—far too loudly, Del thought. "The old savage wouldn't think of touching you. Beneath his dignity."

"Wh-what do you mean?" Del whispered hoarsely. "Y-you don't know sharks, you don't."

"Oh, don't I! Well, I can tell you one thing for certain—that no intelligent, self-respecting shark would dream of taking a boy seriously who could wander about at the bottom of the sea as if he had a perfect right."

Del gazed at him, astonished; and when he looked back again he was just in time to see the tip of the shark's tail disappearing around another bend, towards where all the playful little fish had gone.

"Oh," sighed Coral, clasping her small thin hands together, "I do hope the wee darlings have found themselves good hiding places." And she went paler and paler with fright and worry until she was all the colour of ivory. And it was only when the gay little fish began peeping and flashing about once more with smiles of relief on their faces that she gradually grew bright and rosy again.

Del, too, felt hugely light-hearted now, and quite wildly daring. In fact, for the first time, he felt perfectly at home in this undersea world and went prancing about looking into everything.

Lying at rest in a rocky hollow he found an angry-looking octopus, with any amount of long twisting arms and two wide-

THE CORAL KINGDOM

awake eyes. That gave him a terrible start, and he decided to leave rocky hollows well alone from then on. Turning, however, he saw a great dark gap, edged all round with a wide, vivid purple fringe. It looked very exciting indeed and, almost without thinking, he popped his head right into it to see what there was inside. But before he had seen anything at all, he heard Coral's voice shouting a cry of alarm, and felt himself being whisked out backwards—only just in time to see the great dark gap snap shut, right where his head had been.

He felt himself being whisked out backwards.

"Whew!" he exclaimed, and turned quite pale for a moment, while:

"Look here, how many more times do you think I'll have to save your life before you get home again?" Bushbo asked him, grinning, and still hanging on to the back of his shirt.

"I'm Coral—spirit of the great northern Barrier."

THE CORAL KINGDOM

"Well, I hope you won't go exploring inside a giant clam shell again, that's all."

"Is th-th-that what that is?" Del answered, trying his hardest not to look disturbed. "Is that really a c-c-clam? I've heard about them lots."

"Yes, it is," said Bushbo.

> "And remember, the clam
> Is the chap who will slam."

Coral gave a short, bubbly laugh, then ran round a corner and called Del and Bushbo to follow her, which they did.

"Now this," she said, waving her arm out over a wide stretch of rocky levels and crevices, covered all over with innumerable sea-flowers pulsing with life, each a different dazzling colour and with countless delicate petals—"this is one of my favourite flower beds."

"Gracious!" said Del. "Fancy having flower beds under the sea! And say, they're bonzer, too—lots better than yours, Bushbo," he teased. And, dropping down on to his knees beside them, he touched one gently with his first finger, to see if it was really as soft and frail as it looked. When suddenly, simply dozens of the inside petals swerved in together and clawed his finger for all they were worth.

Giving a startled little grunt, he quickly wrenched his finger away, with the sea-flower's petals rasping to keep hold of it; and for some time after that, he was very docile indeed. Even when Coral showed him her treasure-house of wonderful shells, each the home of a brightly coloured, soft jellyfish just as the giant clam shell had been the home of the fish with the purple fringe —and even when she showed him her vivid pet starfish, gliding over the sea bed just as calmly as real stars sit twinkling in the sky at night-time—Del remained very stiff and polite, giving everything a careful, sidelong glance, but not taking any liberties at all. For he was now quite sure that nothing in the land world was even the least bit dangerous in comparison with anything in the sea world.

But just as he was thinking this more than ever, Coral put her hand on his arm and whispered him and Bushbo to silence, gazing a little distance ahead amongst a group of tall, swaying seaweeds; and there, white and shimmering, tall and very graceful, something was moving—something that, when it

White and shimmering, tall and very graceful.

swept out past them, made Del gasp with wonder. For it was the most beautiful lady he had ever seen—all pearly-looking, with long straight silky hair, and a flowing dress that, as she moved, showed the faintest tinges of many colours. Round her waist was a long silk girdle, and Del could just see the tips of her pearly toes as they skimmed along a tiny bit above the sandy and rocky floor.

THE CORAL KINGDOM

"Glory!" he murmured, quite loudly enough for her to have heard it had she wanted to.

But evidently she did not want to, for she slipped straight past without glancing up anywhere—merely gazing down, with a sweet dreamy smile, at the chubby wee baby she held in her arms.

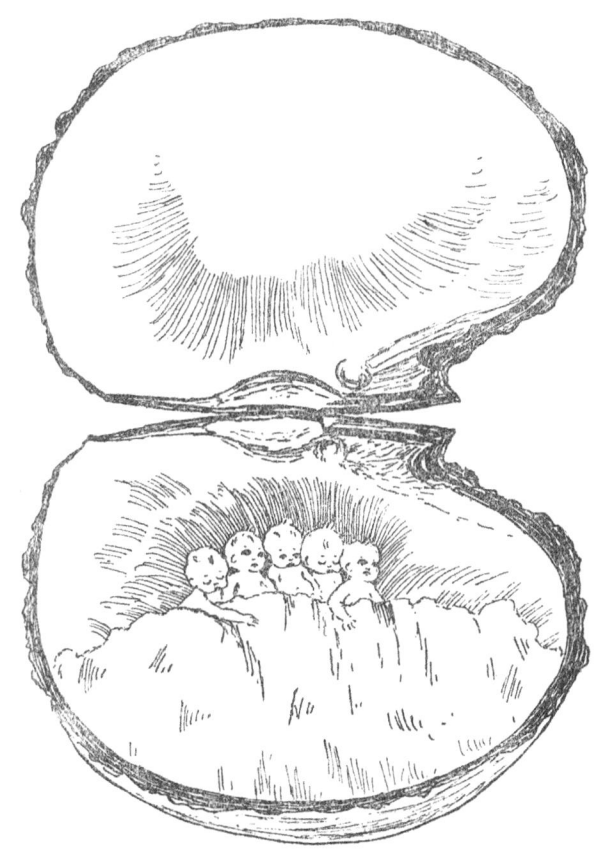

An opened-up shell, gentle and kind-looking.

"Let's follow her!" Del whispered. And all three of them slid eagerly after her on tiptoe.

"But whoever is she?" he asked Coral after a few minutes.

"Why, didn't you see her little pearl baby?"

MAGIC AUSTRALIA

"Yes, but—Oh, heavens, you don't mean that—that her baby was a pearl, do you?"

"Naturally I do. And as for the tall pale lady—well, she's Mother of Pearl, of course."

Del was greatly impressed, but he did not say anything, for now Mother of Pearl, coming to a wide rocky cave, stopped and peeped into it; and he, Bushbo and Coral sidled round quickly to where they could see what she was doing. What he did see, Del was quite sure he would remember for the whole of his life.

There, standing at the edge of the cave, was a large opened-up shell—not cruel and savage like old clam, but gentle and kind-looking—and all inside, the colour of the beautiful lady herself. And there was a soft, billowy quilt lying across the hollow inside of it, and peeping out from under the top of this quilt were five little babies, all bright with a soft, shining whiteness, and all squirming and gurgling with merriment.

Then Mother of Pearl tenderly tucked their wee baby brother in beside them, and they all nestled up happily together. It had been naughty of baby brother to go wandering off into the dangerous sea jungles right at bedtime, and give Mother so much worry finding him. But now all was well again, and Mother was slowly swaying and dancing before them—which was only her way of lullabying them. After this, she lightly touched the tip of the roof shell, and down it came gently gliding, until the cradle was quite closed. And no one would have suspected it of being a cradle now, for it looked merely like two rugged shells clamped up together and interested in absolutely nothing. But Del, Bushbo and Coral knew quite well that there were six shining pearl babies lying asleep inside it.

CHAPTER XIII

OVER THE REEF

"CORAL," Del said suddenly, "have you seen any people like me about anywhere?"

And Coral, now looking like a shy little old lady of misty lavender, stared at him thoughtfully for a moment, then answered, "Well, they do come diving down here sometimes after the pearl babies, but on the whole the floor of the sea is rather a funny place to be searching for them. You ought to go across to the mainland. You'd be far more likely to find people there."

"But how could we get there?" asked Del.

"Yes," said Bushbo, "I'm afraid we're rather duffers at finding our way about down here."

So Coral said she would be very happy to escort them —which she did.

It was a long way they had to travel, through bewitched forests of coral and seaweed, and in and out amongst rocky cliffs and caverns. But there were always so many strange new things and creatures to look at, and the gay little fish who darted about them all the way were so entertaining that none of them grew the least bit tired, even when they found that they had a steep hill to climb.

Up and up they tramped, noticing as they went how the light was getting brighter and more golden, until at last Coral, going a little ahead of them, sprang out with a joyful cry upon one of the many rocks along a beautiful white sandy beach.

"The top at last!" she exclaimed. And Del and Bushbo,

following her up on to what was actually a scrap of the land world, quite crowed with delight to see the sun again, and realized how much they must have been missing it all this time under the sea. But when they turned to share their excitement with Coral, they found that she was looking rather tired and faded, although happy and triumphant too.

"I say, you do look cracked up, Coral!" Del remarked.

"Oh no, I'm all right," she answered brightly. "It's just that I never feel quite comfortable out of the water. So if you boys would like to walk over this island in a straight line from here, I'll slip down under again, and meet you on the other side."

"Oh," said Del, "we haven't got where we were going yet?"

"Dear me, no! This is only one of goodness knows how many islands that I've built all up and down the length of my kingdom. You stroll across it now, and tell me what you think of it." And, with a few circling ripples of laughter, she plunged into the water again and disappeared.

"Well," said Bushbo, "come along. We'd better get a move on."

So, hand in hand, they strode up the beach towards the thick forest of pale, fresh greenness that lay at the top of it.

"Heavens!" said Del. "What a difference! Lovely trees and shade instead of desert!"

And as they stepped into it the forest greeted them with the chattering, warbling chorus of countless birds; for this was springtime, and simply thousands of them who had just come back here after the winter were now enormously busy making love and building their homes, and talking on and on about everything in their own bird language.

Del and Bushbo raced each other through the tall forest of silver-trunked pisonia-trees, laughing and shouting nearly as loudly as all the birds put together, for it was many a long day since they had had a forest to run wild in. So it was no time before they reached the other side, when, dipping down into the water again, they found Coral waiting for them, and smiling all over with a pale golden radiance.

OVER THE REEF

And so they went on for a long while, tramping uphill on to one of Coral's islands, then across this and downhill along the sea floor, until it was time to climb up again on to another island. And always there was the thrill of wondering what the next one would look like, for they were often quite different from one another. Some were covered with pandanus palm-trees, others with pawpaws—and oh, the fun of plunging with both hands into one of the large, soft, golden fruits! Others were masses of rock pools, where all sorts of queer things lived, from lazy sea-slugs lying about on the sandy floor to sharp-fingered crabs who carried about young forests of seaweeds on their backs. And all round the edges would be plants and corals, while pert little fish would go shooting about hither and thither like impish scraps of lightning or rainbow.

Del, forgetting all about the evil-eyed octopus he had met at the bottom of the sea, went feeling round a rock-pool crevice once, to see what he could find, and a great crab shot out and clawed on to his hand. It hurt badly, for its claws were as sharp as knives. But scream and hit and pull and shake as poor Del might, the crab would not attempt to let go. In fact, Bushbo quite had to plead with it before it finally dropped off and, with a sly apologetic grin, sidled back under its crevice again.

"There—there isn't a single nice-natured animal in Coral's whole jolly kingdom!" Del remarked heatedly, after his shock had worn off a little. "Except the little fish, of course," he added quietly.

And he felt like this even more when, dipping deep down into the water again, another huge grey shark came dashing up, and this time charged right into him and knocked him over, then went cleaving on through the water as if nothing had happened. This gave Del an awful fright, and he lay face downward on the sea floor for quite a long time after it, wondering if he could possibly be still alive. But Bushbo's merriment aroused him at last.

"See?" said the golden-brown boy. "I told you no intelligent shark would take you seriously. You'd have been a goner by now if that one had."

So, what with his long walk and several scares, Del did finally grow very tired, and just as he was climbing up on to another coral island he happened to mention the fact, and an old mother turtle happened to hear him.

Now, Del looked a very little boy to be wandering about under the sea so far from home, and Mother Turtle was rather fond of little boys, so, much to his astonishment, she swam out nobly and placed her large self in front of him, with a broad smile on her face. And every time he tried to find his way round her, she heaved over and blocked his passage again, until he very nearly lost his temper. But Coral came to the rescue in the nick of time, and explained what the kindly old turtle had in mind.

"Don't you see, Del? She's offering to carry you across. She wants you to get on her back, and she'll give you a ride."

"Oh, I say!" Del answered, his eyes twinkling. "Would it be all right, do you think?"

"Of course it would, silly! She'd be going ashore in any case round about now, to lay up a store of eggs in some nice sheltered spot, and the kindly old soul wouldn't a bit mind carrying you right over to the other side while she's about it."

After all of which Mother Turtle beamed approvingly; and Del, feeling that this was one of the best larks he had ever heard of, jumped on to the broad brown back without any further ado and was swishing along up to the island in less than a trice, with Bushbo running after him as fast as ever he could.

But then began a toilsome, lumbering journey indeed, for Mother Turtle might have been a champion swimmer, but she proved a very indifferent walker, and seemed to find it so hard climbing up the beach and had to stop so many times for breath that Del at last, with rather a guilty feeling, went to get off. But Bushbo, holding his sides with laughter, made him stay on.

"It's all right, old chap," he said. "It isn't that you're too heavy for her. She goes on like that just the same when she's only got herself to carry. And besides, this is better than a circus any day. Oh my jolly kookaburras, what a joke!"

So Del settled down and let himself be trundled on; for although he hated being laughed at, he could not bring himself to hurt old Mother Turtle's feelings, and he had noticed her expression of deep concern a moment back when he had tried to get off.

However, when he saw that they were more than half-way across the island, with Bushbo teasing and capering along beside them the whole time, he suddenly remembered and, "Hey, what about the eggs?" he asked.

A toilsome, lumbering journey indeed.

At which Mother Turtle stopped and looked round at him with a knowing smile, and Bushbo, with an added burst of glee, asked him what he was thinking of to imagine that such a wise old turtle would let anything in the shape of a mortal boy know where she was hoarding her treasured eggs.

"Oh bother!" Del retorted, drumming his heels rebelliously against Mother Turtle's handsome brown shell. "I *want* to see the eggs. I *will* see them!"

And again the old turtle stopped and looked round at him, this time with a very grave expression, as if to say, "Dear, dear, dear! What a spoilt boy, to be sure! If *I'd* had the bringing up of you, young man, there'd be no such goings on, I can tell you."

Then, turning back once more, she continued her journey towards the sea again—only much easier and faster now, for it was downhill. And when she got to the water's edge, with a great bound and a splash, she plunged in, giving a sudden little buck that sent Del tumbling, rolling and gurgling down, down through the water until at last he landed in a heap on the sandy sea floor, with a bruised head and a greatly injured dignity; while Bushbo ran crowing after him, calling out how that was just Mother Turtle's way of paying him out for his cheek—and oh, what fun it had been! "By all the laughing waterfalls in creation, Del, what fun!"

"And now," said Coral, as they were tramping uphill again after this, "it's time for us to say good-bye, for I've brought you just about as far as I can. But Mangrove will take care of you along the rest of the way to the mainland—if you ask him nicely, that is."

So Del and Bushbo promised that they would ask Mangrove very nicely. But, turning to say good-bye and thank you to their faithful little guide, they were quite concerned to find that she was again looking rather withered and faded.

"Yes," she answered. "To be sure, I have come out of my elements a bit. This water, you'll notice, isn't as clear and fresh as it might be. In fact, it's getting quite muddy—and mud I cannot abide. I really don't know what Mangrove's made of to be able to live in such a mess. He's almost as bad as little boys for liking mud pies."

Then quickly, before she could feel any worse, Coral and the two boys said good-bye, and Coral went back while the boys went on.

The farther they went, though, the nastier it grew, for the water got thicker and muddier all the time until Del and Bushbo could scarcely breathe in it—and oh, how sticky and dirty they felt!

"Coral knew a thing or two when she turned back!" Del snapped, extremely annoyed about everything. "You've just about got to push your way through this jolly stuff, and you can't see two inches in front of your nose in it. Great Scott, why

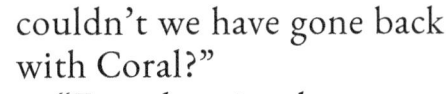

couldn't we have gone back with Coral?"

"For the simple reason that our job's to get on to the mainland somehow, and this is the only way," Bushbo answered, also feeling rather peeved.

"Perhaps, though," they both suddenly heard a slow, deep voice drawling, "perhaps I could make it somewhat easier for you."

And, looking up, they could just see, coming down towards them through the dingy mud, a long branching foot at the end of an even longer smooth, brown leg.

Del gave a small gulp and tried to run, for he did not particularly fancy any such help. But running at the bottom of a mud swamp—especially with no breath to spare—was very difficult; and he had made scarcely any progress when the same slow voice cried:

"Oh come, come! Why are you wriggling so, my little friend?

The long foot had clasped him with two of its branching toes.

MAGIC AUSTRALIA

Don't you know it's hard enough as it is to see what one's doing down there without having one's little friend trying all he can to trick one? Ah, that's better—much better!" he declared at last.

And Del, at the same moment, gave a soft, grunty squeal; for the long foot had found him, and had quickly clasped him with two of its branching toes while, he noticed, Bushbo was lying comfortably next to him, between two more. When he saw this, he tried to settle down and look comfortable too; but his heart was bouncing up and down so fast, and there was such a wild expression in his eyes, that Bushbo burst out laughing at him and told him not to look so alarmed.

Del, however, could make no reply before, with a little plop, the mysterious foot had dragged its two passengers up on to the surface of the mud swamp. And now, for a moment, Del was so delighted at being able to see and feel the shining sun again, and breathe in all at once long draughts of fresh air, that he forgot his nervousness, and even his anxiety to see what the queer creature belonging to the foot looked like.

Then, "Well, of course," drawled the slow voice, with a hint of a smile in it, "no doubt it's a pair of quite attractive young men underneath it all. But just now, I must say it looks more like a couple of outsized mud-skippers."

Del glanced quickly about him in all directions; but the only thing he could see for a few moments was—not far away from him, tightly encircled with twining roots, stretching vigorously, and laughing loudly with Bushbo's own laugh—a tallish boy dull brown and slimy with mud from head to foot.

"Go on! You needn't look so surprised, you great silly!" the boy declared. "You're in quite the same state yourself. And —shivery grasses!—old Mangrove's right. I've never seen anything that wasn't a mud-skipper look more like one."

And just then a real mud-skipper went skipping past over the entanglement of branches and roots that covered the swamp, and Del stared indignantly at the large-headed, bulging-eyed thing, half fish half lizard, then cried out, "Mud-skipper yourself!"

OVER THE REEF

At which Mangrove—wherever the fellow was—gave a slow, deep chuckle; and Del, scratching his head, gazed round everywhere in search of him. Funny, he thought, being held like this in a chap's toes and not having any idea of what the chap himself looked like. And then suddenly, when he was least expecting it, he did see him, and he got such a surprise that he sprang right out of Mangrove's grip and tripped face downward into the mud again, so that had Mangrove not stretched his little toe out and levered him gently up, he would certainly have sunk to the bottom again.

"Oh heavens! Oh my heavens!" Del exclaimed, and stared and stared. For Mangrove was positively covered with noses—narrow, bluntly pointed affairs, with small round patches all over them, so that they looked like sponges. There was a string of them right down the centre of his face, from the top of his forehead to his mouth; and there were any amount of them drooping down from his arms, and even some standing up from his legs.

Del was quite shocked—and looked it.

"Well," said Mangrove in his calm, lazy manner, "you've been down there. You ought to know how hard it is to breathe in solid mud. If you had to live in it all your life, you'd grow a lot more than one nose, too—in the parts of you that weren't buried. And what's more, you'd also see that they were made nice and spongy, so as to be able to soak up all the air possible." But Del was not a scrap sure that he would. And Mangrove's slim bent body, and grey-green hair, and thin arms and hands, and endlessly branching legs, all shook with laughter.

"Well I never!" Del cried out, looking his great tree friend up and down again and again. "Do you have to have dozens and dozens of legs, too, Mangrove—as well as noses?"

"Our young mortal here," Bushbo brought in, smiling, "doesn't know the first thing about politeness."

But Mangrove did not seem to mind this, and before he answered he carefully set the two boys down on a supple woody hoop, which was really one of his branching legs. Then, "Yes, my lad," he said. "I do indeed have to grow dozens and dozens of legs—as, again, you would yourself if you had to spend your whole life in all this loose stuff. Why—in the name of mud and moving tides, my boy—how do you think I could ever keep my balance if I didn't spread out everywhere gripping on to as much as I could? Two little spindle legs like yours would be a lot of help, wouldn't they?"

But just the same, Del was quite sure that nothing on earth could persuade him to grow dozens of legs any more than it could to grow dozens of noses. For deep inside himself he thought Mangrove quite one of the ugliest creatures he had ever seen—which was rather a pity, since he seemed so kindly and to have so many hardships to struggle against.

Bushbo, however, was now looking wistfully into the distance, beyond the wide stretch covered with Mangrove, to the solid land. "That," he said, pointing, "is where Del and I are wanting to get to. But it looks pretty hopeless, O Mangrove —unless you help us."

"Help you?" Mangrove repeated, slowly closing one eye in his narrow, angular face. "Why, my dear lad, of course I'll help you." And after a long, deep chuckle, he gave his leg a jerk that sent the two boys spinning.

Up into the air they went, just as if they were being played football with. Then down, down they came, somersaulting on the way.

"Ow!" Del screamed. "I'm falling!"

"How—very odd!" Bushbo remarked, breathlessly.

But just then they landed on something, and this gave a little beneath them before sending them spinning into the air once more. And so, on and on they went, nearer and nearer the shore, Mangrove having the game of his life catching them on one foot and tossing them across to another, and chuckling the whole time like bubbling mud. Every now and then they caught

OVER THE REEF

a glimpse of his beaming face amid the regular forest of trees they seemed to be whirling through, but mostly they saw only a haze of dull green and a bewildering tangle of branches. Once, desperately, Del caught hold of a fairly stout trunk and tried to cling on; but this turned out to be Mangrove's waist, and sent the fellow into such a fit of ticklish giggles that Del was jerked off more abruptly than ever.

So that the two boys were mightily relieved when at last, with an extra-strong throw and an extra-merry chuckle, Mangrove hurled them right across on to the rugged sandy shore.

"Oh gracious! Oh gracious alive!" Del muttered, tumbling over and over, and feeling as if he would never stop.

And Bushbo, also tumbling, felt very much the same. "No doubt about it," he declared at last, sitting up and holding his head in his hands, "Mangroves a strong, springy fellow all right."

And then, giving his head a good shake and blinking, he stared out towards where they had come from, and Del did too; but neither of them could see anything except a huge mud swamp covered all over with a hopeless tangle of grey-green trees.

"Fancy all those legs!" Del said seriously, after a moment. "And great Scott," he added, still more seriously, "all those noses, too!"

CHAPTER XIV

THE WIDE AWAKE DREAM

DEL and Bushbo kept sitting there for a long time, chiefly because they were too tired, after their journey across Mangrove's swamp, to do anything else. And finally, still feeling very tired, they realized that the sun was setting, turning the sky into the vividest flame and gold they had ever seen. Even the beach they were sitting on shone golden. Then everything began to get dark. In fact, in the twinkling of an eye everything *was* dark; and Bushbo, lying straight down on the sand, was asleep the very next moment. Del knew he was, for when he asked him something there came no answer except the light, smooth sound of his asleep breathing. And as this made Del himself feel tireder than ever, it was no time before he was fast asleep too. Then, immediately, a strange, beautiful dream came to him.

It was a lady—tall, golden-brown, stately—gliding towards him over the sea. She was bright and fresh as the dawn, and her dress was a floating cloud of golden gossamer, and her deep copper-coloured hair was heavy with waves and wispy with little curls. Around her head was a trailing strand of wattle with, in the very centre, a flashing jewel—flashing with all the brightest reds, greens, blues and yellows that one could ever find in the petals of flowers or the wings of tropical butterflies, or in the lights and dancing of Opal. And now, as Del remembered that tricksy little spirit girl of darting flame, even though only in a dream, the old pain at having lost her came back to him. Then, however, he thought of the opal-magicked cockle-shell in his pocket, and realized that he did have a tiny scrap of her after all

THE WIDE-AWAKE DREAM

—which made him happy again as, awed and wondering, he kept watching this beautiful dream lady who seemed golden-brown all over.

There was even a pendant of solid gold around her neck, and a glowing brightness shining out from her as if she were a lamp. But—strangest thing of all—although there was no wind, her long hair kept billowing up rhythmically around her head like an untamed forest of moving waters, flashing and shimmering

Magnificent and ancient one.

continually into a curious form; into the shape of the prettiest map in the whole world, his own Australia. And, gazing at her, Del thought she must have been alive a long time, for although in a way she seemed very very young, she also looked so wise and gentle. But she was a lot more too. In fact, she gave Del the feeling that she was everything at once— everything he had seen and felt and lived since that morning so long ago when he had wandered out of Uncle Edward's little wooden gate and strolled along the bush track to the top of the mysterious cliff. She was all of his marvellous surprises, friends, adventures, joys, fears and queer little sadnesses.

Del felt suddenly so lost and tongue-tied that he could only stand gazing in silence, and wishing that Bushbo would turn up from somewhere—which was exactly what Bushbo immediately did. And the wonderful golden-brown spirit seemed just as delighted to see him as Del was, for, holding out her arms to him, she cried. "Come! Oh, come to me, my gallant, gentle-hearted little Bushlands—you who cover my east with life and beauty!"

And Bushbo quickly obeyed, running up and resting his hand confidingly in hers, and gazing up at her with deep, affectionate eyes. "Everywhere I can, O magnificent and ancient one," he replied.

"True!" answered the glowing spirit. "But come, my Eastern Bushlands and my mortal youth! Now that you have glimpsed the hidden wealth and life throughout my desertlands, come a little westward and explore the lush fertility of my central north, and marvel even more!"

Then suddenly she was no longer there, but in her place were the soft fires of dawn, spreading over the sky and lighting up the whole earth. And Del, for no reason at all, felt so free and thistle-downish that it almost seemed as if the air had gathered itself into a wind under his feet, and lifted him with it high up towards the few thin clouds, then playfully pushed and tumbled him on with—yes, with Bushbo beside him, westward, away from the dawn; always westward.

Even at the time, as often happens, Del knew quite well that he was asleep, and, glancing across at Bushbo, he said, chuckling, "Stupid things dreams are, aren't they?"

THE WIDE-AWAKE DREAM

And Bushbo, looking at him a little strangely, replied, "Yes, they are, rather."

However, stupid or otherwise, this was certainly great fun—this soft tumbling and gentle floating way up in the air—and, for as long as it lasted, Del enjoyed himself immensely. But of course, it did not last for ever. When finally the wind subsided, Del and Bushbo subsided with it, gliding down, down, like two little silken parachutes, until they landed in a great open country of tall, husky grasses and thin ragged trees, and above all of huge buildings.

Real dream buildings, Del thought, gazing at them. No sense in them whatever. They were mostly a sort of grey-red-brown colour, and were all kinds of different shapes and sizes. Some were smooth and rounded; others had towers rising high, high up like the towers of ancient castles. Some were rough and knobbly, as though hobgoblins lived in them; others were slender and graceful, as though they had been built for dusky little nymphs. But none of them was like anything that Del had ever seen before; and clearly there was not an atom of reason or use for them, scattered about like this all over scrubby grasslands—which was, of course, quite in keeping with their being only dreams. And he was just going to lean across and tell Bushbo so when, in a tremendous flurry, a long-legged, much-befeathered emu came striding past with a haughty and preoccupied expression on its face, and made such a bustle that Del and Bushbo both woke up with a start, Del gazing about him, quite bewildered; for this was not the sort of thing that should happen when one woke up from a dream. The dream itself should not go on exactly the same as before. Yet here he was, rubbing his eyes and blinking; and there, making off into the distance, was the striding emu; and all around him were the same dozens upon dozens of queer-shaped buildings.

Bushbo, however, was not looking the least bit surprised. "Well," he remarked, springing to his feet and stretching, "here we are—just where she advised us to come—in her central north."

"But—but look here, Bushbo!" Del exclaimed. "I'm all mixed up about things again. D'you mean to say that—that all that was real, and not a dream?"

"What you don't seem to have found out yet, little white mortal one," Bushbo said with a smile, "is that the things you think of as dreams are very often real, while lots of the things you're sure are real are only myths and fancies."

"Oh bother! How on earth do you ever know where you are in this place?" Del demanded hotly. "And anyway, who's 'she'?"

"Why, surely you knew her!" Bushbo replied, looking shocked. "How could you mistake the spirit of your own golden land?"

"Yes, well I did know really," Del protested. "But I just wanted to make sure. Same as I'd like to know about all these funny things here—who made them, and what they're for, and why they're here, and—and why they look so silly."

"Silly!" Bushbo repeated. "You wouldn't think they were silly if you were a tiny white ant, old chap."

"Why's that?" Del asked. "What have white ants got to do with them?"

"They live in them, that's all. And they've built them, and they're mighty proud of them."

"Heavens! If I'd heaped up such a clumsy-looking stack of mud, I wouldn't be specially proud of it—and I certainly wouldn't live in it."

"Ah, but that only proves you're no white ant," said Bushbo with a grin.

Del strutted over to the one nearest him and, after looking it up and down several times, gave it a scornful kick, expecting to see the whole thing crumble to bits, although it stood more than twice his height and goodness knows how many times his width. But he saw nothing of the kind. Instead, he only gave himself a very sore toe, while the queer building took no notice at all. So, round and round he hopped on one foot, making a wry face.

THE WIDE-AWAKE DREAM

"Well," said Bushbo, laughing, "it serves you right for attacking them without reason, old chap. And by the way," he added, "that's one of the reasons why they're so proud of their good work, those millions upon millions of tiny white ants; for what they've built themselves are not only homes, but real fortresses. You'd just about have to get an axe on to them to break them up."

"Anyway," Del answered, pouting, "I didn't attack it. I was only having a joke."

"—and I certainly wouldn't live in it."

"Come on, then!" said Bushbo. "Let's wander up north a bit farther, and see what's to be seen." And he gazed about him at the miles and miles of flat, dry grasslands with a scattering of light gum-trees over them.

"No," said Del, chuckling. "Only these busy White Ants, eh?"

So, on and on they walked, over the hard earth and the dry crunching grasses, with the giant white-ant homes standing about everywhere like grim, silent castles, and the gum-trees sprinkling them with flakes of shade. Every now and then a brightly coloured parrot would fly screeching past; and once or twice a big grey kangaroo came vaulting and thumping along and, catching sight of the two boys, stopped for a moment all alert, with pricked ears and keen eyes and little folded-up front paws, then turned and sprang off in the opposite direction. Once they came upon a company of long-legged, stork-like birds, called brolgas, holding a dancing court in the middle of the plains—bobbing and strutting and curtseying all together in perfect formation, and looking most quaint with their demure grey feathers and serious expressions. But apart from this, nothing happened. It was a long, dreary journey of unending sameness; and at last Del plomped down on the scorched grass and announced that he was hot and was going no farther. But Bushbo, as soon as the rustling sound of their footsteps had stopped, heard something else and, hushing Del, asked if he did not hear it too.

Del listened and listened, and then—sure enough—floating towards them through the still, hot air, he heard one of the sweetest voices in all the world. It was so frail and clear that he could almost see it—transparent, lissom, quivering; a formless something, singing its song of pearliness and coolness in the burning heat of noon.

"Say, Bushbo!" he cried out and, no longer tired, ran eagerly towards the sound, with Bushbo beside him.

The farther they went the clearer they could hear it. It did not grow any louder—merely became more pearly and more transparent. And at last, there it was right beside them. Surrounded with what even Del felt sure must be a magic circle —a circle of gum- and wattle- and tea-trees—was a large, still lagoon, covered all over with waterlilies of every colour: cream, pink, yellow, blue, red, mauve. Del could scarcely believe that it was true, and, forgetting to wonder about the singing, stood

THE WIDE-AWAKE DREAM

gazing open-mouthed at this garden of beautiful flowers.

But Bushbo seemed to have seen something else for, waving towards the centre of the lagoon, he cried out, "Hail, Waterlily! Your shining, liquid harmonies have called us from far out over the kingdom of grasses and white ants—called us to your watery haunts in the centre of a dry wilderness."

And Waterlily made no answer that Del could understand,

Enfolded the lagoon in a shimmering caress.

but the singing seemed to flow out into a smooth, clear sheet; and, watching hard, he thought he saw a pale, trembling, cloud-like figure of blush-coloured ivory half rise from the water and stretch out her slender arms until they seemed to enfold the whole lagoon in a shimmering caress.

MAGIC AUSTRALIA

Bewildered and quite spell-bound, he closed his eyes tightly for a second or two, then opened them suddenly again. But now, gaze as he might, he could see nothing except a floating garden of waterlilies, shining in the sun.

"Oh Bushbo," he whispered, "did—did you see anything just now? Or did something go wrong with my eyes?"

"You great silly, Del!" Bushbo answered him, ruffling his hair and laughing. "Won't you ever get used to us? Why, I dare say you'll be asking me one of these days who *I* am—or even, perhaps, *if* I am. Of course there wasn't anything wrong with your eyes. That was the beautiful spirit of waterlilies, who hovers over so many of the lagoons up here in Australia's north."

CHAPTER XV

THE COUNCIL OF ELDERS

AFTER this the two boys travelled farther north for quite a long time and, coming to a little trickle of water, followed along beside it until it had spread out into quite a fair-sized river, flowing between banks richly covered with plants and shade. Then, in a particularly wooded part, Del and Bushbo both stopped suddenly, for a curious hush seemed to have fallen all around them—the kind of hush that made them feel they must have interrupted something. Del was very puzzled at this; but Bushbo seemed to know all about it, for he glanced up quickly at one after another of the great trees towering all around him, and gave a short burst of laughter which was echoed by a kookaburra high up somewhere—as it had been once before that Del remembered—and cried out:

"O mighty and majestic elders, continue your council! The little one here is our friend."

Immediately there came a jagged sort of rustling, and Del, looking up, saw a tall pandanus palm shaking its wild, tufty leaves about. This seemed very strange, as there was no wind at the moment and all of the other trees were quite still. But then, as he stared more intently, he saw something even stranger. Below the great tuft of leaves there were actually two round, bright eyes, a pointed nose, and a thin mouth that, smiling, showed a row of tiny, even, saw-like teeth.

And before Del had time to say or do anything, the whole tree bent down slightly and, in a keen-edged voice, declared, "He may be our friend for now, in that case."

"Hello new friend, then," stated a new voice—a slow, heavy,

The Council of Elders.

THE COUNCIL OF ELDERS

twining voice, which gave Del the odd feeling that it was folding itself about him and clinging on as if it never meant to let go.

And, wheeling round abruptly, he saw a huge banyan-tree with a fierce, misshapen face hardly visible in the shade of its dense leaves, and with heavy twisting arms and legs that looked exactly like the sound of its voice. Not only this, but Del was shocked to find that some of its arms had folded right round a young gum-tree near by and seemed to be strangling it. Flaming with indignation, he marched over to Banyan, clenched his hands against his hips and, glaring up defiantly at the grim face, cried out, "Hey, you! Look out! Look at what you're doing! Wh-why don't you pick on someone your own size?"

But Banyan only yawned, looked extremely bored and slightly amused, then answered slowly, "Of course, my boy, it's a matter of opinion whether it's so bad to strangle a useless young gum in the cause of one's own mental and physical support."

"Now, don't take any notice of his nasty expression, little mortal," brought in a sweet, half-whistling, reedy voice. "What he says might be true enough, but he's got such an unpleasant manner—poor dear!—that he's likely to make things sound quite horrid."

And Del, spinning round towards where this music-making creature seemed to be, stared for quite a long time amongst a clump of now giggling bamboo before he saw, nearly at the top of one of the smooth round sticks, a most comical face that looked as if it was all made of half-moons, with dipping half-moon eyes and a great dipping half-moon mouth that, for all Del could see of it, might have gone right round the stick in a complete circle.

"Great Scott!" he murmured. And he stood rigid, looking so thoughtful and solemn that suddenly there was an enormous shuffle of laughter from every direction at once, in an endless number of different tones and keys, and Del hopped round so quickly and so many times, trying to see what all these creatures looked like and where they all were that at last he flopped down on the ground, very dazed and giddy indeed. Whereat the laughter rang out more hilariously than ever, and Del felt quite mortified about it.

But then, even more loudly than all this deafening mixture of noise, "Silence!" boomed a deep, vibrating voice—a voice that seemed to be echoing back through goodness knows how many millions of years.

And immediately there *was* silence.

"This," continued the voice, "is most unseemly conduct for a council of dignified trees."

"Now," said Del, springing to his feet again and rushing over to a clump of giant fronds, that this new voice seemed to be coming from, "where and what on earth are *you*?"

But he had only just finished saying this when he hopped back a step and, very uncertain of what he should do or say next, peeped out of the corner of his eye through a tiny gap between the fronds; for what he had caught a glimpse of inside there had set him wondering a good deal. It was a large, stern face that looked extremely ancient, all brown and dull green in colour, except for a flash of red in its eyes; and it was made of a great number of scales, overlapping one another and each sticking straight up into a sharp spike. Del had never seen anything quite like this before, and he was not a bit certain how far he should trust it.

But he soon found that he had nothing to fear from it, for, lowering its voice to a rumbling murmur, it replied, "What am I, young mortal one? Macrozamia is my name—son of that noble and ancient family of Cycads which has been living on this earth for millions upon millions of years. Ah yes, there are few to-day as ancient as I—few who, like I, still live in fact instead of only in memories; in mere leaf-prints left down the ages within hardening rock."

"In other words," Bushbo whispered, having come up beside Del, "he's really one of those living memories we were talking about that time with Desert Pea."

THE COUNCIL OF ELDERS

"Well, to come back to the subject," crinkled the crisp, papery voice of nearby Tea-tree who, though hung all over with ragged strips of bark, was very slender and elegant and had a sweet, almost girlish face with soft grey eyes, "what can the spirit of life and growth achieve even here in the tropical north, if humans are so challenged by the strange unreasonableness of the rain sprites and the river spirits?"

"Ah," drawled a voice Del clearly remembered—the voice of Mangrove—as that many-nosed creature of muddy tastes thrust one twining foot up above the surface of the slimy river edge.

"Ah, there lies the root of the whole matter."

"Where?" Del demanded, looking hard at Mangrove's foot.

"In," explained the dry voice of stately Gum, standing on the outskirts of the gathering, "in the unreasonableness of the rain sprites, diving down all over us in their millions for five solid months of the year, then deserting us entirely for the other seven months. No sense in behaviour like that."

"And," solemnly added Macrozamia the ancient, "in the headstrong nature of the river spirits who now, at the very end of the dry season, are fooling about doing practically nothing—in some parts actually lying dry-asleep—whereas in the wet season of the rain sprites' visitation they gallop along their tracks like wild things and, not satisfied with this, rush out from their own domains in roaring floods and invade all the country round-about, drowning as many people and animals as they can, and uprooting as many honest plants."

"Well, but look here," Del remarked wisely, "can't you *do* anything about it?"

"I," whistled Bamboo, "certainly keep track of as many rain sprites as I can, to tide me over the 'dry'. But I can only save enough for myself, I'm afraid, so don't really do very much."

"I too," Banyan coiled in with a sly glance over his great, powerful self, "have plenty of room for housing rain sprites—for my own use, that is."

MAGIC AUSTRALIA

But Del refused to take any notice of Banyan, and was just about to change the subject curtly when Macrozamia the ancient boomed out, "In short, little mortal, we plants have all done what we could in our own ways to make life more possible for ourselves. But alas, it is still a hard life."

Then came an uprising of a great wind, which grew wilder every minute, blowing Del and Bushbo and the trees almost inside-out, and darkening the sky with great fleets of the blackest clouds Del had ever seen.

"The beginning of the 'wet'!" sighed all the trees together, gazing up thirstily at the sky. "The beginning of the 'wet'!"

Whereupon Del, forgetting his newest likes and dislikes in trees, and bolting up to where he saw the most shelter, which was under the heavy leaves and amongst the twining hanging arms of Banyan, cried out excitedly, "Heavens, what a bonzer storm we're going to get!"

And he had only just said this when down they came —shouting, riotous, diving swarms of rain sprites, the same as he had seen in the desert. Only now there were so many of them and they were coming down with such force that he could scarcely pick out one from another, and if he quarter closed his eyes, he could see nothing except a solid sheet of shining whiteness. It was all great fun, he thought, chuckling and murmuring away to himself, and glancing across at Bushbo who was sheltering inside a curtain of bamboo; for now he knew so much more about rain than most people did, that it was wonderful to make himself see it as the rest of the world did and as he himself had done until not long ago. And he was thinking so much about this and so little about anything else that he got a tremendous shock when suddenly he felt a long hard something wrap around him and heard a slithering voice above him remark:

"Now, young man, you'll learn to be grateful to me and not behave so rudely towards me!" And there, to Del's horror, was the corded, tangled-looking face of Banyan, smiling slyly down at him.

THE COUNCIL OF ELDERS

Overhead screeched a flock of parrots.

"Ow! Help!" he screamed, and, with a jump almost as big as a kangaroo's, instantly sprang clear of Banyan's enfolding arms and legs and ran over to Bushbo through the wet, pounding swarms of rain sprites, dizzy and sick-feeling with fright.

But Bushbo, placing a gentle arm around his shoulders, laughed good-naturedly. "Poor old chap!" he said. "You do get a rough spin, don't you? But Banyan's all right really—an awfully fine fellow in his own way. You mustn't feel like that about him."

"Well, I—I do," Del retorted, "and—and I always will. So there! And I'm getting out of this place as fast as I can."

With which he turned and ran with all his might, the fierce wind blowing against him and the rain sprites landing heavily all over him. And of course, there was nothing for Bushbo to do except run after him, along the river bank, over the quickly rain-sodden earth.

"Valleys and precipices, Del!" the bush boy called out. "I've done absolutely nothing, since I first met you, except chase and rescue you. When are you going to give me a rest?"

But Del did not answer. He merely ran on, the river beside him growing larger and flowing faster the whole time, until it really did seem to be galloping, just as Macrozamia said it did in the season of the rain sprites. And the forest bordering it, instead of growing thinner the farther he went, grew steadily more and more thick, with twining creepers tangling themselves together from tree to tree, and lovely flowers hanging down in heavy strands from high branches. Real orchids they were, such as Del had only ever seen before in pictures and hot-houses —never growing wild like this.

At last Bushbo caught up and, grabbing him by the arm, asked. "What on earth do you think you're doing, little silly, flying about like a mad thing?"

But Del was too out of breath to answer, and merely stood choking and coughing.

"Upon my sunny word, you're the easiest chap to scare I've ever known," Bushbo added, with a broad smile.

Del looked indignant, but could think of nothing proper to reply, so merely walked along sedately beside Bushbo for some time. And then just when the rain sprites seemed to be diving down more furiously than ever, suddenly there were no more of them and, gazing about in astonishment, Del could see nothing except flecks of golden sunlight twinkling through the tangled, flowery forest.

"Well I'm blest!" he declared and, wandering slowly down to the muddy river edge where any amount of fallen logs were lying, sat down on one of them to think things out, when:

"Trees and mountains, boy!" Bushbo shouted. "Look out! Quick!" And he came rushing down so fast that he nearly tumbled over head-first on top of him. Instead of this, however, he made a wild grab at the neck of his shirt and snatched him away like a whirlwind, just as there was a terrific snap right beside him.

"Oh heavens! Oh my heavens!" poor Del exclaimed, turning very white and feeling all whisked up inside; for, glancing quickly round to see what had snapped, there, only a few inches away from him, was a huge hungry-looking crocodile—with gaping jaws now, ready to snap again. And this, he realized with horror, was the log he had sat down on. And not only this, but it was merely one of absolutely innumerable logs. The whole

THE COUNCIL OF ELDERS

muddy, oozy river bank was covered with them, and every one of them was a crocodile, and each of them looked hungry, and had the evillest glinting eyes and the widest snapping jaws imaginable.

The log he had sat down on.

Del was so terrified that he stood where he was, quite stiff, and had no idea of how to make himself move. And still, there in front of him, were all the crocodiles, gazing at him and licking their chops and making ready to glide up and gobble him whole, for so dainty a morsel as such a little boy they had not tasted for many a long year.

"Del, you little ass, what's the matter with you?" Bushbo screamed and, grabbing him bodily under one arm, scrambled up the slope with him as fast as a startled possum, until, safely out of reach of the savage brutes, he stumbled over face-downward on the wet grass, and Del with him.

"A good solid weight of mighty stupid boy!" he panted.

But Del was far too relieved and grateful to answer back, and while Bushbo was still not looking he actually blinked away a few aching tears; then, sitting up, touched his golden-brown friend rather timidly on the shoulder.

CHAPTER XVI

FOUND!

NOW that the rain was over and the sun was out again, everything got very hot and steamy. After the many long months of dryness, every plant large or small—and indeed the whole earth—seemed to be lifting itself up with a strange kind of soft heaviness, which was both murmuring and fragrant, and made Del extremely drowsy. Several times he had to shake himself hard to stay awake; but even then his eyelids kept drooping, making him see things misty when they were solid, double when they were single, and moving when they were still.

So, when a wavering grey-brown cloud, vaguely human in form, seemed to rise up from the ground in front of him and drift backwards and forwards slowly, smoothly, lingeringly, he at first did not think of believing it. But soon he found that the harder he shook himself and the wider he opened his eyes the clearer he saw it. And, to be sure, he had met so many queer things since Bushbo that this was not, he realized, so very strange after all. So he sat quite still watching, and wondering what might happen next.

For a long time, however, nothing happened—nothing, that is, except floating and wreathing and swaying. Then at last, the spirit creature reared itself up, up, higher and higher until Del thought it might touch the very sky, when, slowly, it came sinking down again, with a faint breathing sound. And now it was that, feeling through his whole being this deep sigh of the earth spirit, Bushbo sprang to his feet and gazed before him, which Del immediately did too.

"Oh, kind and generous Earth," Bushbo greeted the strange

FOUND!

being, which now hung there with downcast head and eyes, and heavy with a hooded grey-brown mantle, "why do you sigh thus sorrowfully at the coming of the rain sprites? You should be filling the air with smiles and gaiety."

But Earth only sighed once again, even more deeply than the last time, and murmured, "Ah, little bush spirit from the mild

Not quite liking to go any farther.

east, how can I be glad when all my bountifulness is of no avail —when what I give to-day is stolen to-morrow; when what to-day I grow is to-morrow destroyed?"

"But—but how? Why?" Del asked, strutting forward a step or two, then not quite liking to go any farther. "Who steals and —and destroys it?"

"Daly," sighed Earth. "Daly the merciless." And the shrouded spirit cast a backward glance over its shoulder towards the rushing river swarmed all over its banks, as Del and Bushbo shudderingly remembered, with crocodile logs.

"What, you mean the old crocs chew everything up?" Del asked.

"No," answered the spirit sadly. "It's Daly himself. The rain sprites excite him so much that I'm afraid he grows arrogant beyond all reason in the months of their visit—and savage and full of destruction. And, bursting over his rightful banks. He uproots every bit of my good work, and carries it away or drowns it."

"For don't you see?" suddenly came a great bellow that gave Del a frightful shock and nearly deafened him. "I am the master spirit of the central north!"

And when this shout, with all its throbbing echoes, had faded far away through the jungle and left the whole place in silence, except for the headlong rushing sound of the great river not far below, Del and Bushbo found that the shrouded earth spirit had vanished, and that there were only drifting, heavily fragrant clouds of steam rising up from the ground.

"Heavens!" said Del.

But now again, all of a sudden and with even more vim than before, the rain sprites came plunging down. And every moment they seemed to gather themselves into thicker and heavier swarms, pounding on to the two boys—even through the jungle of palms, ferns, vines and trees—until they both felt sore all over. And the farther they walked on and the faster the sprites fell, the louder roared the river and the nearer to them it seemed to surge. So that at last, when they came to a bend and found themselves almost on top of the water, Del was not as surprised as he might have been at what he and Bushbo saw there.

Rising up haughtily in front of them from the surface of the dashing water was a shaggy, lion-like head of liquid brown, with

FOUND!

eyes that were usually closed but which, when opened suddenly now and then, lit up with lightning streaks of every colour imaginable: the green of the jungle, the blue of kingfisher wings, the red of parrots, the white, flame and purple of tropical orchids and butterflies.

"Daly!" Bushbo whispered, stepping up closer to Del.

But he could say nothing else before, with a darting outward fling of a brown, raggedly liquid arm, the solemn river spirit

Del was not as surprised as he might have been.

caught up the two boys into a spinning whirlpool that tumbled them about almost as roughly as gay old Finke had done, and then landed them safely, though extremely breathless and dizzy, in the very middle of his streaming mane.

"Come!" bellowed the same lionish roar they had heard a few moments back. "Now that my power is greatest—when the rain sprites are re-awakening in me the mightiness that is mine—come with Daly the great one, and see, see his power!" And onward, with the ferocity of ten vast thunderstorms, hurtled the proud Daly, every second going faster and spreading wider and shouting with greater volume.

But somehow or other, Del could not take him seriously. He could not make himself feel properly. He remembered back, back—ever and ever so far—to his lively surprises and terrors in Willie-willie's wind chariot, to his eagerness when meeting Broome, Baobab, Spinifex, Desert Pea, Coral. He remembered how many times his heart had pulsed and bounded in the underground palace of Nullarbor; how he had trembled all over with fright amongst the heat tribes, on the ghost of Lake Eyre, in the whirling bag of old Dust-storm, after his narrow escapes from the octopus, the clam and the crocodiles. He remembered how he had loved Macdonnell Ranges, that generous green giant of sparkling waters, singing birds and priceless wealth; how he had pitied Water, the beautiful prisoner of the underground; how his whole self had ached with sorrow at Opal's mischievous vanishing; and how, with wonder, he had scarcely dared breathe at the beauty of Mother of Pearl and her shining jewel babies, or later at the glory of that golden dream lady—"magnificent and ancient one", as Bushbo had called her—or at the misty brightness of the waterlily spirit. And he remembered, too, how keen about everything he had been, all those seeming ages upon ages back, at the council of elders—of mighty trees—into whose midst he and Bushbo had stumbled.

Yet, try as he might, he simply could not take Daly seriously. No matter how often he had to wriggle himself free from the twisting, watery strands of that lion-like mane, and no matter how furiously the great river rushed on or how loudly he roared and boasted, still Del simply could not make himself feel anything: only a drowsy befuddledness, much as he had felt just before the rising of the earth spirit.

This was extremely upsetting, and poor Del, struggling amid

FOUND!

the entanglement of old Daly's mane, tried harder and harder to wake himself up again. But it was no use. He could not even see anything clearly. There seemed to be a cloud over his eyes, so that jungles, and emerald-coloured grasslands, and jungles again —everything went streaking past as if in a dream; and even Bushbo looked far away and misty.

"Oh Bushbo, Bushbo!" Del suddenly cried out. "What are you doing with yourself? Don't go away, Bushbo—please!"

But Bushbo's only reply was to smile at him in that gentle, affectionate way Del remembered from several times before, and loved so well.

Indeed, there was hardly a chance for any further answer, for now, slowly and laboriously, old Daly was snuffling his way out to sea through a swamp of solid mud and, instead of being entangled in a clear, watery mane, the two boys found themselves hopelessly bogged; and not only this, but surrounded on all sides by swarms of slimy crocodiles even more hungry-looking than the first ones.

Yet, so dazed and stupid did Del feel, that even these fellows did not particularly disturb him. And the next moment he was glad he had not wasted any energy getting panicky about them, for, just as he might have guessed, jolly old Mangrove had come to the rescue, and was once again having the time of his life bouncing the two boys about from one twining, springy foot to another, right up, along the coast, towards the peak of Australia's central north.

Oh, thought Del, yawning and giving a little stretch, it was all very pleasant. Nearly sent a chap to sleep. And he even forgot to worry about the mistiness over his eyes or how far away everything seemed.

But finally the whirling and bouncing stopped and he found himself standing, with Bushbo, actually upon solid ground.

And now, to be sure, something did startle him awake for a few moments, for here was one of the strangest and most beautiful sights he had ever seen: a tall, untamed man figure, golden-brown the same as Bushbo, only long-haired and bearded. And his hair and beard were streaming with rain and wind as he stood there on the sheer edge of a precipice, with up-flung head, gazing out upon the tossing, stormy ocean. And Del could see only about half of him, for he was standing amid a jungle heavy with scent and colour: a wild entanglement of white, purple, red, blue and yellow flowers, with coconut palms and huge dark trees rising up among them, and with every now

A tall, untamed man figure.

and then the spasmodic flight of a jewel-like bird or butterfly shooting between them a thread of even more brilliant colour.

But it was the man figure himself that Del thought most wonderful of all; for, though untamed and solitary, he also looked very gentle. And, deep inside him somewhere, Del had a longing that was almost a pain, to creep up through the hibiscus

FOUND!

and the frangipanni and the golden cassia and, nestling his head against that great brown chest, stay there for ever and ever. Even now as he thought of it he could almost feel the man figure's strong arm fold around him and hold him close, close, in that scent-laden warmth and all-moving stillness. Yet he did not seem an altogether happy spirit as he stood, powerful and silent, gazing out to sea. There was a look of suffering and hunger in his eyes—of desolation that went strangely with the colourful luxury of everything around him.

Then Bushbo, seeing the puzzlement on Del's face, explained to him. "You see, he's only just now reviving, Del, and drinking deeply of what the rain sprites are giving him, after languishing in dryness and thirst for the past long months. Darwin is his name, Del, and he is one of Australia's finest and wealthiest towns."

It was all very dream-like, Del thought, and somehow very beautiful, with the rain sprites plunging about everywhere in their millions, and the masses of flowers weighing the air down with their fragrance, and Darwin standing nearly shoulder-deep among them, and Bushbo's musical voice.

Then, with a suddenly welling heart, "Oh Bushbo," he said fervently, "I could do it all myself. I can feel it inside me somewhere. Oh, it's—it's almost too big for me, Bushbo. I feel as if I ought to be ten thousand giants all in one to be able to hold it. It—it feels like all the power in the whole world—like a great rushing wave lifting up inside me and driving, driving, driving me—"

"Del!" Bushbo broke in, his eyes—indeed, his whole self—seeming to light up with a strange, golden fire. ""Oh Bushbo, I mustn't forget this. I mustn't forget it ever—ever!"

Then it seemed that the hand on his shoulder strengthened its touch into something like a grip; when suddenly, with eyes as wide-awake and bright as Bushbo's, he looked up, smiling, at the golden-brown boy beside him. And there, gazing down at him with a serious, worried expression, was—Uncle Edward.

Del's joy changed to utter dismay. "Gracious!" he exclaimed. "Gracious alive! " And then he merely stared and stared.

"Well, sonny, to put it mildly, I'm the one who ought to be saying that," his uncle declared, gently turning him away from the little wooden gate he had been leaning over, and leading him up the path towards the house. "Your dad and I have been noticing you through the window off and on for ever so long, hanging over the gate here as if you were in a dream. Then I thought I'd better come out and see what you were up to—and, upon my word, sonny, what's all this talk about Bushbo? What on earth *have* you been dreaming about?"

"Oh, but Uncle Edward, I *haven't* been dreaming. I haven't!" Del told him impetuously. "It was the realest thing I've ever known. I've seen where Water's imprisoned and the spirit of life and growth in the Desert. And the palace of Nullarbor, and Macdonnell and Flinders Ranges, who simply piled us with treasure. And the central north, with more of the rain sprites and sand tribes. And old Daly rushing up over everything every now and then and messing up all the work of the earth spirit."

"Yes, my boy, you're quite right there," said Uncle Edward, although he was looking more and more puzzled every minute.

"And now tell me, who's this Bushbo?"

"Bushbo?" Del repeated, raising his voice excitedly. "He's the best pal ever. He's a bonzer chap."

"But—well, where do you find him, sonny?" Uncle Edward persisted, scratching at the back of his head and frowning.

And for a moment Del said nothing, but also only scratched at the back of his head and frowned. Then, his face brightening, he answered, "Why, he's everywhere. Everywhere round here, that is. He comes up to you through the tea-trees, with the sun shining all over him in tiny gold pools. And you can hear him laughing with every waterfall and kookaburra, and see him smiling in every wild flower."

FOUND!

Then, suddenly thrusting his hand into his pocket, he felt a wonderful collection there of things he had quite forgotten about; and, with a gurgle of delight, he now drew some of them out and arrayed them on his hand, right under Uncle Edward's nose. "See?" he cried out, twinkling. "Macdonnell Ranges gave

As if he were in a dream.

me those—and those. And he gave me lots more, too. And Spinifex gave me that. See the gold in it? And—and this," he added more quietly, picking out the opalized cockle-shell and handling it fondly, "this is the home of a little fish who lived

MAGIC AUSTRALIA

thousands of years ago, and—and Opal cast her spell over it so that it would last for ever. Desert Pea told me."

Uncle Edward was quite silent for a few moments after that, and so was Del. Then, putting his arm about the little lad's shoulders, "Come, sonny," he said. "Come inside and tell me all about it. Every word, mind you—right from the very beginning."

And, overjoyed with himself and everything else, Del skipped along in front of him into the house, feeling quite sure that Uncle Edward was the best uncle in all the world.

THE END OF THIS MAGICAL TALE

IN OTHER WORDS—

HERE, again, are some of the queer things and people that Del met on his travels with Bushbo—first (*in slanty print like this*) as Del himself saw them, and then (in straight-up print like this) as grown-ups think of them. All of which is just to show other boys and girls one way to play at grown-ups—that is if they feel like it.

Bushbo. The bushlands along Australia's eastern coast, green and gracious with trees and ferns, colourful with myriads of wild flowers, gentle with the caperings of little soft furry animals, musical with bird songs.

Willie-willie. The aborigines' name for the great hurricane of electricity, wind and rain that blows in from the sea with the north-west monsoon during the summertime, and ravages Australia's north-west coast. Many times it has been known to blow whole towns away, while the willie-willie'd sea has a record of almost countless drownings to its name. Similar hurricanes also occur in Australia's north-east where, among other things, they make the Great Barrier Reef far more dangerous than usual for men to navigate, and play havoc with its coral.

Broome. Australia's most important pearling town, situated on the north-west coast. Before the war it was mainly inhabited by Japanese, who seemed better trained than others in the strenuousness of diving. The diver's life is a trying and dangerous one, although the thrill of finding precious pearls must make up quite a lot for his fear of cramp, sharks and other perils.

Baobab. A tree of often clumsy form and of seemingly endless life (even safe from white ants), that befriends people in the dry north-west. Apart from its edible seed-pods and fever-curing

MAGIC AUSTRALIA

flower petals, it stores water from the rain times in its knobbly crevices and spongy pith, while the enormous hollow trunks of older baobabs have often been used as homes by lonely wanderers. Some of the inside "walls" of these are grooved all over with the names, initials and stories of people who have inhabited them.

Desert. Abject dryness and barrenness, thought to extend over huge sections of Australia's interior. In almost every instance, however, underground water is revealed with only a little tapping, while many parts are studded with permanent springs and soaks. And always, after rain, even the driest parts of the so-called desertlands are transformed into green and flowery wildernesses.

Spinifex. A hardy, wiry grass with spear-like leaves, and roots that spread wide and dig deep. It grows over enormous tracts of Australia's dry sandinesses, including most of the parts where gold has been found. Its widely clinging roots do much towards fixing the sand from being blown about in raging wind-storms, and, while providing food and shelter for many small living creatures (rabbits, bandicoots, lizards, snakes, pigeons, beetles), it is also the friend of people. The aborigines have long made use of it in their home (mia-mia)-building and for fishing nets and gums, while others have even built strong roads with it.

Mirage. One of the loveliest if most distressing features of the desert. Mirages are merely reflections of the sky which look like a lake in the far-off flat sand, which acts like a mirror. Many a time has a parched and starving traveller run wildly towards a lake of cool, blue water shimmering in the distance, only to find the same infinite sands—and death. The salt lakes in South Australia are likewise haunted by mirages, which even occur over the coral reef off the North Queensland coast. You can even see such mirages in far-off flat roadways, which also act like a mirror even though they are black when you look straight down at them.

IN OTHER WORDS—

The Conquest of the Rain Sprites by the Sand Imps. One of the main reasons for the dryness of Australia's sandy interior. Water sinks more rapidly through sand than through any other type of soil; so rain, in most of the interior, soaks down beyond the reach of plant roots almost before they have had time to avail themselves of it. What the sand does not bury, the hot sunrays dry up.

Water. One of Australia's several great artesian or underground basins of water. In certain parts rain water, having soaked through to almost spongy rocks under the earth, is stored here in great quantities and, if a bore be driven down into the basin, will rush out boiling hot. Tasting strongly of minerals, men find it nasty to drink, though it may be good for cattle.

Macdonnell Ranges. A very extensive and fertile group of mountains, hills and valleys in Central Australia, rich in mineral wealth, rivers, pasturelands and fauna. It is here that the famous Finke River rises and Palm Valley lies. In this valley grow some of the finest and most ancient palms and cycads in the world. Another notable feature of these ranges is the "ghost" gum-trees: tall, handsome eucalypts whose trunks are "whitewashed" with a powdery substance that brushes off when touched.

Desert Pea. Sturt's Desert Pea, brilliant red, usually with black marking, which grows widely over Australia's more southern desertlands. It runs flat along the ground and flowers profusely.

Ghost of the Inland Sea. The memory of prehistoric days when a great sea flowed through the centre of Australia, from Spencer's Gulf in the south to the Gulf of Carpentaria in the north. Many proofs of its existence remain to this day, including gibbers (water—rounded stones), the salt lakes, fossilized and opalised shells, and sometimes whole opalised skeletons of prehistoric sea creatures.

The Opal-magicked Cockle-shell. Australia being the oldest country in the world—that is the country which has stood for the longest time above sea level—has particularly interesting fossils. Indeed, were it not for this country, many such records of prehistoric plant and animal life would have been entirely lost to man. There are parts of Australia's desolate sandy and rocky reaches which are strewn with these tangible memories of the world's infancy, some of them from immeasurably long ages before the birth of man.

Dingo. The only wild dog in the world, who howls instead of barking, has been thought to hunt sheep, rabbits and other prey with the slyness of a cat, and is sleek and powerful in build. Owing to their being thought of as eating farmers' sheep, people have been paid to hunt dingoes, and in the "puppy season" the people of Oodnadatta have made a handsome living by trapping them. This is a pity, for, apart from its uniqueness, the dingo is the most intelligent of all Australia's animals. Also, it has been found that in fact dingoes eat mainly insects such as grasshoppers rather than farmers' animals.

Finke. The oldest river in the world, and one of the most beautiful, which rises in the upper Macdonnell Ranges and flows through deep rocky gorges, and valleys gloriously vegetated —mostly with palms, cycads and gum-trees. When it enters the lower ranges its flow is much interrupted, though permanent springs and waterholes mark its course. But it is mainly quite a dry riverbed over the desert between the foot of the ranges and its destination (Lake Eyre), its huge dry bed of dazzling white sand silently telling the story of its prehistoric riverhood. To-day it is only on rare occasions of particularly heavy rainfall that the Finke, flooding, rushes over its desert bed, its waters always, however, mysteriously disappearing as it enters Lake Eyre.

Ghost of Lake Eyre. The largest of the mystery salt lakes in South Australia. It is always dry, no matter how much water might flow into it from flooded rivers. Many people have tried to cross it, but no one had succeeded in doing so when this book was first written. Its infinite expanses of mere brine and

IN OTHER WORDS—

mud (hundreds of miles across), no less than its cruel mirages, had defeated people every time.

Dust-storm. Rushing, whirling winds that lift everything in their way—particularly the tractless sands—and cause frightful devastation to any attempts at human settlement in that sunken region of dry lakes and rivers between Flinders and Macdonnell Ranges, and south-west toward Nullarbor Plain.

Opal. Quite one of the most beautiful gems in the world, and Australia's national stone. Australian opals may be so much lovelier than any found in other countries. It has been found around the joining-up part of Queensland, South Australia and New South Wales and, by its erratic behaviour, casts a spell over its miners such as do few other precious stones. It follows no logical rock course or "reef". Often not a glint of it is to be found where it seems most likely, whilst thousands of dollars' worth might turn up suddenly when least expected. Few miners, once they have seen the flash of opal, by candlelight in the dark underground, can ever give up their search for it. Inside, opal is made up of billiions of tiny quartz spheres, all stacked together in beautiful regular arrays of blocks, each containing thousands of spheres, which diffract rainbows of light out in many directions when a beam of white light enters them.

Flinders Range (which Del did not see, you will remember). Extremely rich in minerals and as sheep lands, and very beautiful for the daring colour contrasts in its bushes, rocks and sand, this range of hills and mountains lies near the top of Spencer's Gulf. It is already studded with sheep-raising settlements.

Nullarbor. A 650-by-720-kilometer expanse of sand, stones and saltbush in South Australia's south-west and Western Australia's south-east, crossed by the trans-continental railway. Only comparatively recently has it been found that Nullarbor Plain is really the roof of a huge maze of underground caves, perhaps not as beautiful as the Jenolan Caves of New South Wales, but far more interesting for the naturalist, and rich in mineral wealth. Under the plain there are also known to be long, icy-cold rivers. As yet the exact nature and extent of the caves are unknown, only a few of them, accessible through blowholes, having been explored.

Coral. The substance of the Great Barrier Reef, which extends for 2000 kilometers off the coast of northern Queensland. Countless thousands of years have gone to the building of the reef, with its innumerable islands and coral varieties—as may well be imagined when we learn that coral is made by millions of polyps which are small animals that live and work in close association with one another. They often have even tinier little creatures living inside them that convert sunlight into energy for them both to use. It seems that ever since the dim long-ago when a large section of Australia's eastern coast sank beneath the sea, these little coral polyps have been intent on building it up again. The rock-pool and undersea gardens of the reef, with their corals, fish, crabs, sea-flowers, -stars, -slugs, -weeds, might be counted amongst the prettiest things on earth, and include amid their teeming life much that man has not as yet found or classified.

Clam. If a giant clam manages to catch a head, arm or leg, it will probably never let go, so divers must be careful. The clam fish however, which protrudes along the opening of the shell in brightly coloured fringes, makes the trap so conspicuous that people do not often "fall into" it.

Mother of Pearl and her Pearl Babies. Pearls, the "precious stones" of the sea, are abundant on the Barrier Reef, as they are off the coast around Broome; and the shells in which they are formed, though covered on the outside with drab greyish crusts, are solid nacre or mother of pearl inside. This sun-, moon- or rainbow-shine nacreousness belongs to many others besides pearl-shells—particularly trochuses—and has been in great

IN OTHER WORDS—

demand for the making of "pearl" buttons, buckles, studs, inlays, cutlery handles and so on.

Mother Turtle. A lovable feature of Barrier Reef life. Mother turtles make a habit of going ashore to lay their eggs some time in the spring, and are as noted for their clumsiness in walking as for their nimbleness in swimming.

Mangrove. A tree which inhabits enormous tracts of mud-flats, mainly around Australia's north-west, north and north-east coasts. It grows an entanglement of supple branching and sub-branching roots, which grip the mud over large areas and thus keep the tree supported in its soft medium and against the movement of the tides. Often its branches and roots develop smaller "breathing" roots whose sponginess draws in large quantities of air, to make up for the airlessness of the mud. Along some parts of the coast there are veritable mangrove jungles.

White-ant Homes. Great structures, built by countless millions of termites or white ants which live by eating wood and which men therefore regard as frightful pests. A termitarium is as strong outside as it is complicated inside, where it is one great mass of rooms, corridors and galleries. There are all shapes and sizes of termitariums and the one Del kicked goes up high as the tree it has eaten, cascading down in muddy-brown folds to the ground. The strangest kind of termite mound is the very thin greyish-coloured "magnetic" one which looks like half of a disk sticking up from the earth, up to 2m high, whose ends always point north and south while its sides face east and west, giving the termites a fairly constant temperature all day long from the sun's rays, which don't hit much of the mound at midday but warm it nicely in morning and evening. These termite homes form a special feature of the bush of the Northern Territory and North Queensland.

Pandanus. Usually known as the "screw-palm", this ragged tree grows abundantly in the northern parts of Australia.

MAGIC AUSTRALIA

Sometimes it forms dense jungles and, its leaves being prickly underneath, such jungles are most uncomfortable to travel through. Many people find its fruit unpalatable, but aborigines do eat it.

Banyan. When it grows to its full size, a huge tree with dense dark foliage, and aerial roots that hang down from its branches and sometimes twist around the trunks of smaller trees, eventually killing them.

Bamboo. A light, graceful plant which, however, in some parts of the Daly River country, grows into jungles almost impossible to penetrate. The aborigines cut spears from bamboo stems, and also didgeridoos, which make a deep and resonant melodious music.

Macrozamia. Not a tree-fern, as it is often thought to be, owing to its general appearance, but a cone-bearing plant (of the cycad group) which is one of the most ancient in the world. In most other countries it has long been extinct, only fossil remains of it existing; but it still flourishes in many parts of Australia, particularly the tropic north. Its seeds turn brilliant red when ripe.

The Earth Spirit. The fertile soil of the tropical north, which has shown itself capable of growing anything that people might try in it, from peanuts to maize and cotton. With proper precautions against drought and flood, and with established regular and adequate means of transport and communication, the entire north has been thought to be able to be a wonderland of industry, production and wealth. Many have tried to do this but the remoteness and weather have defeated most attempts.

Daly. A great river of the north, with crocodile-infested mud-flats at its mouth and along much of its course, and noted for its jungle-like surroundings and its capacity for ruthless floods; so that while it gives life, it also takes it. Great peanut plantations are only some of the many things that have thrived around it; but, owing to transport and other difficulties, the farmer's life there continues to be fraught with trouble.

IN OTHER WORDS—

Darwin. The port of the extreme central north of Australia. Languishing in terrific heat and thirst by the end of the "dry", it is regularly transformed by the five months' wet season into a fairyland of luxuriant growth and colour. Large barren tracts become emerald-coloured pasturelands, and from end to end of it there is, as it were, a carnival of tropical flowers, while brilliant-winged butterflies and myriads of other insects would provide a lifetime's study for any keen entomologist. Darwin in the "wet" is a veritable spell-weaver, where nature's generosity runs riot and human industry is so often defeated.

www.ingramcontent.com/pod-product-compliance
Lightning Source LLC
Chambersburg PA
CBHW081356290426
44110CB00018B/2399